Acknowledgments

I wish to thank the following people for their inspiration and other support in creating this book. First, I'd like to acknowledge my devoted sister whose assistance and support at every stage, especially as we wrestled with the first manuscript, was extremely valuable. I am also thankful to my editor and friend, not only for her professional assistance with the manuscript but also for her enthusiasm, which gave me the courage to move forward when the project seemed stalled.

To my friends Lucas, Alex, and Darrin goes a special 'thank you' for their editorial assistance and unbiased comments. Any errors are my own and should not tarnish the reputations of these people. In addition, I am grateful to the family who provided the opportunity for me to experience healing in their garden sanctuary in Central America. The first draft of this book, handwritten, was born there. To others who have loved and supported me despite the rollercoaster nature of my disability, thank you all. One day soon, our heavenly Father will reward you.

From the Editor

"A butterfly in a bear's body." Some days, that is still an accurate description of myself – the times when my energetic preference to *flit* battles against my lethargic need to *sit*. Some days, the little girl in me who longs to skip and jump feels caged inside a weakened body.

I spent years under a dark cloud of guilt. The resulting workaholism led to burnout, apathy, and depression. Truly a 'blue butterfly,' I existed in bear-like hibernation long after winter was past. But thankfully, more recently, I have wanted to sing more than cry – I have renewed H.O.P.E.

The Heaven-sent assignment of editing the manuscript of this book was a healing balm to my weary soul. While reading it, I discovered in its pages that I was not the only person in the world with the experiences transparently shared by the author. Though my struggles did not include premenstrual dysphoric disorder (PMDD), I could indeed relate to many of the issues described.

No longer feeling alone, my façade – the mask that was nearly permanent from decades of wear – began to melt. Relief filled my heart as a triple burden was lifted off my shoulders – the world I thought I could carry, the shame I thought I *should* carry, and the fear of being crazy.

This book has given me the courage to emerge from my self-spun cocoon and live joyfully for our Creator. May *Shine for Me, Blue Butterfly!* do the same for you.

No longer blue,
C.J. Marshall, Editor

Please feel free to copy, reproduce, and distribute any portion of this book, including on the internet, under the following three conditions:

1. The information must not be altered in any way.
2. The title and publishing information must be included.
3. The reproduction must not be done for profit.

Disclaimer:
The information contained in this book is intended to provide helpful information on the topics discussed. This book is not meant to be used, nor should it be used, in the diagnosis or treatment of any medical condition. If the reader needs expert assistance, the services of a skilled professional should be obtained.

Email: colormax.creations.2024@gmail.com

For permission to reproduce the information in this publication for commercial redistribution, please email the above address.

All Scripture quotations are taken from the *World English Bible*, Public Domain.

Published 2013 by Bookpatch.com
Republished 2024 by Draft2digital.com

©Brenna Hasheider
All rights reserved

In memory of my mother,
who introduced me to my Creator,
and in memory of Alex, my travel angel.
Thank you both for *shining*.

Foreword

I would like to introduce you to my friend and associate, Brenna, a genuine and sincere woman who strives for a life of structure and a character that God approves of. Brenna lights up the room when she walks in and has a presence about her that demands the floor. These are two aspects of her personality that I have had the privilege to enjoy for two years as we worked together in my health and healing spa.

During that period, I witnessed the dark side of Brenna's life that increased over time. I repeatedly observed her mood swings, the sudden 'Dr. Jekyll and Mr. Hyde' performance that could take her out of the scene at any moment without warning.

Even with the massive steps forward in her general health, the mystery of Brenna's mood swings and depression remained. Eventually, she took the opportunity to live at an isolated garden retreat on a mountain in Central America. Daring to take that step provided one of the final pieces of the puzzle in living with cyclical depression.

There in the jungle, the storm clouds lifted, leaving her free to finally begin living out her purpose, and she started writing this book. Living in a crude shelter in the jungle so she could work on this book, she returned to civilization once every week or two just to replenish her raw food supply. To my amazement, she handwrote the manuscript for *Shine for Me, Blue Butterfly!* in a few short weeks in that healing mountain sanctuary. Once she saw the light, there was no holding her back.

You may be deep in the dungeon of depression as you hold this book, but please take courage. Read just one paragraph at a time if necessary, or read one page if you can. As dark as the maze of your life may be now, reading *Shine for Me, Blue Butterfly!* will start you on a path to seeing yourself in a new and brighter way as you rise above depression, despair, and darkness and begin to shine, not just for yourself, but also for the world around you.

Let Brenna be your friend as you read about coping with the symptoms of PMDD. Brenna's valiant struggle against the devastating symptoms of this disorder is an example of recovery from a life of...well, you must read her story to know what I mean about leaving the darkness and entering the light. She has been there and can be an inspiration to you as she has been to me.

Darrin K. Poitras
Author of *Divine Power, Human Strength: 10 Master Keys to Ultimate Health and Mind Success*
Winnipeg, 2012

Contents

Shine for Me, Blue Butterfly!

Premenstrual Dysphoric Disorder (PMDD):
A Survivor's Journey

Brenna Hasheider

Introduction

In today's world, it seems that everywhere we turn – the Internet, TV, books, or elsewhere – there are stories of people living with 'invisible disabilities' such as chronic fatigue syndrome, epilepsy, and fibromyalgia as well as those who have survived life-threatening illnesses such as cancer, diabetes, and heart disease. Yet how often do we hear about women battling severe depression, fatigue, irritability, anger, suicidal thoughts, mood swings and other debilitating symptoms monthly and their struggle to keep living?

I have suffered from premenstrual dysphoric disorder (PMDD), a severe form of female depression, most of my adult life. When I was 44 years old, I finally realized that my symptoms were cyclical, meaning they followed a precise pattern. The weepiness, lack of energy, rage, suicidal thoughts, and desire to harm myself appeared and intensified 7-14 days before menstruation every month, and the symptoms abruptly vanished within a day or two of getting my period.

According to recent statistics, there are approximately 31 million women (3-8% of menstruating women) in the U.S. and Canada alone who impatiently wait for their monthly menses because they suffer from PMDD. Getting their period can mean the end of two weeks of misery and the beginning of two weeks of so-called normalcy.

Who can benefit from this book? If you suffer from PMDD, or any other form of depression for that matter, I am confident that my story will motivate you to stay in the battle.

Husbands, brothers, sons, and other family members of those who suffer with PMDD and depression, you are on my heart also. Within these pages, you'll gain greater insight into how to relate to depression and the many people who suffer from it.

However, this book was written with a special compassion for the women who can truly identify with my story, women who will not meet my cry for compassion with blank stares and unresponsive silence but who can sympathetically empathize because we are in the same (often capsizing) boat. These women know what it feels like to be swallowed up in the cold, dark waves of depression. I know there are other women who share a similar experience. We are 'soul sisters' traveling the same, or at least a similar, road.

This is a book of some of my memoirs, but names and identifying details in personal stories have been changed to protect privacy. I have endeavored to share only those details that I feel are essential to understanding the extent of my struggle with PMDD and the damaging influence it has had on my relationships.

We are all human; we all have faults and frailties, and it is not my intention to point fingers at anyone except myself. These memoirs were written purely from my perspective. I have dredged up dim details and timeworn conversations from my unreliable, disease-distressed memory and recorded them as best I can.

Every good story has a hero, and my story is no exception. In writing this book, I found that I needed both good guys and bad guys, supermen and scoundrels, to reveal the most accurate and comprehensive picture of my journey. Therefore, I have chosen Alex to represent the heroes in my life and Lucas to represent the scoundrels.

I wrestled long and hard with the focus of this book, whether to keep it general, since both men and women alike deserve the same hope that there is a better day coming, or whether I should concentrate more on women's depression, specifically on PMDD. One day as I was writing (and drinking deeply of my rich healing environment in Central America), a large butterfly elegantly fluttered in front of me, blindingly blue against the tropical green foliage. It was truly the most spectacular butterfly I had ever seen.

"Blue women are like blue butterflies," I thought to myself, "just waiting to have the opportunity and environment to fly. Though we might be depressed (have the blues), we can shine like these stunning blue butterflies." So, my dear sisters, this book is especially for you.

The Eternal God says, *"You are the light of the world. ...Let your light so shine before men, that they may see your good works and glorify your Father who is in Heaven." (Matthew 5:14, 16).* He says, "Please, my daughter, my son, I need you to shine for Me and for the rest of the world."

Brenna Hasheider
Central America, 2012

Author's Postscript: This book was written prior to menopause, magnificent menopause, after which life began for me. Almost overnight, my dark gray world turned to color and the birds began to sing on a more regular basis. Only the grace of the Eternal One carried me through the darkness to see and hear the beauty of His creation now, and I am filled with joy and gratitude.

"Yahweh, you have searched me,
and you know me.
You know my sitting down and my rising up.
You perceive my thoughts from afar.
You search out my path and my lying down,
and are acquainted with all my ways."

Psalm 139:1-3

Chapter 1 – Why I Needed Hope

Making the Connection to PMDD

A new friend of mine (who does not have time for trivial chats) recently asked, "So what are some significant events from your life's journey? I want a bulleted list of all the highpoints."

His request, though outwardly simple, was complex. "Well, um, you see…" I hesitated. "That's a tough one." After a few awkward moments, I rattled off the following information in chronological order:

"I was raised in a single-parent home with three older siblings, earned a few degrees, worked a rich variety of jobs, survived an apartment fire, taught English as a volunteer in Asia for several years, married twice, was divorced twice, cared for my mother the final two years of her life, and helped a husband build a house."

Recalling my two failed marriages and multiple moves, I hung my head in shame and said, "A perfectly lovely life record, isn't it?"

"That is exactly what I asked for," he replied. Then he added with a smile, "Thanks. That was a whole lot easier than looking at faded photographs for two hours on a Saturday night!"

As I reflected on the list, I realized, not for the first time, that my life to that point had been relatively worthless. "If I die today," I thought to myself, "what would I have to show for my life on Earth? I have been in and out of relationships, in and out of countries, and in and out of rented rooms and apartments. I have spent countless hours deciding whether to leave unhealthy relationships; and then when I finally *did* decide to leave, I have had to figure out *how* to leave in the most peaceful way possible without financial or social support. I have followed my mind in crazy circles of thought and cast shadows on the pathways of others."

These were not exactly things that I'd be proud to present to the Eternal God on Judgment Day, but this little exercise did help me realize how much of my life had been consumed by my battle with PMDD. Losing two weeks out of every month to its symptoms made my life's journey considerably painful and exhausting. Even so, I do not regret that I have had to suffer from the effects of this illness because of the deeper spiritual experience I have gained as a result. The Eternal has blessed me with a firm faith in Him, a profound need to cry out for strength outside of myself, resulting in a deep dependence on His divine power that I might not otherwise have. For these gifts, I will be eternally grateful.

Gratitude aside, how many times have I found myself in a difficult situation, a tight spot, with my face to the wall and seemingly nowhere to turn? Like Job in the Bible, I have complained bitterly, *"He has walled up my way so that I cannot pass, and has set darkness in my paths. He has put my brothers far from me. My acquaintances are wholly estranged from me. My relatives have gone away. My familiar friends have forgotten me."* (Job 19:8, 13-14). Nevertheless, my heavenly Father has *always* provided a way out, often at the last minute, but He has always rescued me.

In the Beginning

"Are you sick?" my mother asked for the umpteenth time when she saw I was still crying. I was 13 or 14 years old and had been sobbing uncontrollably most of the day.

I shook my head 'no'.

"Do you hurt somewhere?" she persisted.

"No," I answered between sobs. "Only in the depths of my heart," I added to myself.

"Do you have cramps?" she inquired.

Again, I shook my head. "No."

"Did you get a bad grade on your algebra test?" she asked, still trying to come up with a logical reason for my endless weeping.

"No!" I wailed again, wishing she would stop probing but not having the energy to articulate the words to ask her to do so.

Finally, exasperated, my mother left the room.

Is It Them or Me?

After I went away to college, I still had an abundance of weepy days and weeks, but I usually blamed them on boy-girl issues or lack of sleep from living in a dormitory or countless other reasons. However, the bigger problem at that point in my life was my frequent touchiness over seemingly insignificant issues, like who was using shampoo from the bottle I had left behind in the dorm shower, or why the girls next door were blaring their music past midnight.

I assumed my problem was a character weakness that I needed to conquer. Half a dozen failed relationships later, including two marriages, I was still asking myself, "Why am I so crabby and irritable sometimes? Is it them or is it me?"

But the most distressing symptom (which grew worse year after year it seemed) was bursting into tears for no apparent reason on any given day and then crying for days on end, as much as two weeks out of every month.

Friends would say, "You're just sad because things did not work out in your marriage. You'll heal faster if you cry. It's normal." Or they might say, "You have every right to lose your temper. Look what he (or she) did to you!" Or "It's just your hormones." Well-meaning people told me, "This is a normal part of being a woman. You just have to grin and bear it, my dear. We each have a cross to bear. This is your lot in life, your thorn in the flesh."

Sometimes I believed them, not knowing what else to blame it on. I tried my best to cope with a "suck it up" attitude, a stubborn strength inherited from generation after generation of German ancestors. Like so many other women, I simply came to accept my mood swings as an inevitable part of womanhood – a part of "the curse." But surely, God did not want me to be miserable 180 days out of 360, did He?

A Stranger Named PMDD

My heart cried out to the Eternal God again and again, "There is nothing normal about spending two weeks out of every four feeling exhausted and irritable and weepy!" My heart was screaming, "This is not right! This is not normal! Something is very wrong. This is not just *me* losing my temper or thinking about killing myself or hitting myself on the head because I hate myself. *Someone else* is in my body. It's a stranger doing these things, thinking these thoughts."

I definitely did *not* want that stranger around. She was messing up my relationships, stealing my happiness, and taking away my peace of mind. In frustration, I tried everything from prayer to Prozac to get rid of her so I could live life instead of wishing I were dead most of the time. Finally, at age 44, I learned *she* has a long name – premenstrual dysphoric disorder (PMDD) – and she has visited me nearly half of every month since I began menstruating at age 11. I know there are other women who can identify with my agony.

Making the Connection

Through the years, I have tried everything I can think of to help myself feel better when the symptoms of PMDD are tormenting me. Finally, one day during an argument, my husband said observantly, "You're a real witch, you know? You pick fights and cry for days without any reason to *the week before you get your period*."

Thinking he was talking about PMS, I insisted there was absolutely no connection between my behavior and PMS. Afterall, I had never suffered from any symptoms of PMS that I was aware of except for monthly cramps. Besides, I thought PMS was supposed to last only a few days. Though his remark offended me at the time, I will be forever grateful for his astute observation because it caused me to pay more attention to my monthly cycles. That was all I needed to make the connection.

After tracking my moods for the next three months, it was obvious that there was a *very direct* correlation between my moods and my cycles. How could I have been so blind all those years, thinking the problem was simply a case of my bordering on insanity (or at least feeling like I was)? What a relief to know there was a "real" reason for my mood disorder, a biological one! When that critical connection was finally made, I felt like climbing to the top of the nearest mountain and shouting, "Hey, world, I am *not* crazy! My neurotransmitters are just messed up!"

PMDD and Relationships

PMDD has a devastating effect on relationships. Considering my numerous failed relationships with men over the years, I believe it's appropriate to include something about a few of these relationships in this book. In spite of allowing myself to be the victim of several men – to be abused, sexually harassed, molested, abandoned, and controlled financially and socially – I have other male friends and teachers for whom I have great respect, so this book is not "male-bashing." I struggled for months, even years, with each decision to stay or leave the unhealthy relationships. In every case, I stayed long after the relationship had ended.

I sometimes wonder if things might have worked out differently had I (and my partners) understood PMDD. For example, *what if* my moods had been more even and I had been cheerful instead of sad and irritable more days than not? *What if* I hadn't lost my temper and lashed out, calling one of my men a hypocrite when I was angry one day? *What if* he hadn't threatened to kill me for saying that? *What if* he hadn't put his hands around my throat to choke me?

What if I hadn't asked my man to bring me a blanket when I was crying and cold and had had enough energy to get a blanket for myself? *What if* he had shown some compassion and had brought me a blanket instead of ignoring me and continuing to play his computer game? *What if* he had treated me like a princess as he vowed he would when he married me? Enough *what-if's*. PMDD had a significant influence on my relationships.

I think of the words to a poem written by Margaret Snell Nicholson, a woman who suffered from four incurable diseases:

Treasures

One by one He took them from me,
All the things I valued most,
Until I was empty-handed;
Every glittering toy was lost.

And I walked Earth's highways, grieving.
In my rags and poverty.
Till I heard His voice inviting,
"Lift your empty hands to Me!"

So I held my hands toward Heaven,
And He filled them with a store
Of His own transcendent riches,
Till they could contain no more.
And at last I comprehended
With my stupid mind and dull,
That God COULD not pour His riches
Into hands already full![1]

A Dilemma

Living with fire-breathing dragons was another stressful dilemma for me. These dragons were men who turned into raging bulls if I crossed them. Here's the scenario – you've spent half the day preparing a full-course dinner that you think your husband will enjoy, and when he gets home from work, he looks at the food on the table that you've worked so hard to make delicious and attractive, and he states bluntly, "I'm eating out tonight."

Maybe he invites you to go along to the restaurant; more than likely, he does not. Moreover, when you show that you're tired and upset, explaining that you'd rather eat at home, his face turns red with rage and his eyes bulge as he yells, "How come you never want to eat out with me? Go ahead. Stay home by yourself. I'm going out!" He leaves, slamming the door behind him, leaving you standing there

------

[1] Brown, Josh. *"In the Midst of Pain."* Feb. 26, 2007, www.mercydrops.com/Snell.htm. Accessed June 17, 2012.

alone in tears, wondering what you did wrong and why he is mad at you.

"I didn't serve the right food," you think to yourself. "No, that's not it. Maybe it's too early and he is not hungry. Or maybe the food is too hot." You'll probably never know the truth, so you put all the food you prepared for him into the refrigerator for another day and then proceed to devour three peanut butter and honey sandwiches (or a bag of chips or a pint of ice cream, your favorite comfort food).

Was I afraid of dragons with violent tempers? Yes, for several reasons. One was because of my poor self-worth. I assumed that a man's rage meant I had done something wrong, that he did not *approve* of me. Because I could not live with their disapproval, I did everything in my power to *earn* their love, forgetting the important fact that if people do not love us for who we *are* instead of what we can *do* for them, then they do not love us at all.

Another reason I feared dragons is that in a moment of anger, they can lose control of themselves and go temporarily insane. One of my men was specially trained in the elite forces of the military; he was trained to kill. (Is it any wonder that a depressed woman often cannot see the way out of a dangerous relationship?)

There were two important healing components missing for me: a healing and supportive environment and an opportunity to get out of the messes I kept creating.

"Yahweh is near to those who have a broken heart,
and saves those who have a crushed spirit.
Many are the afflictions of the righteous,
but Yahweh delivers him out of them all."

Psalm 34:18,19

Chapter 2 – My PMDD Symptoms

For me, the acronym PMDD stands for "**P**lunged into **M**enstruation's **D**eepest **D**arkness." Who are the many visitors who possess my mind and body every month? They are my five 'friends' Weepy Wanda, Irritable Iris, Fatigued Francine, Raging Rhonda, and Harmful Hannah. Wanda, Iris, and Francine visit the most; but Rhonda and Hannah are never far behind.

Fatigued Francine

Chronic fatigue syndrome affects thousands of people in today's society. Perhaps you suffer from it yourself. This is a debilitating kind of fatigue that disrupts and unbalances lives. For me, fatigue meant simply that – severe tiredness or exhaustion. It would pounce on me like a cat on a mouse. I never knew when it would hit, although I learned to recognize the occasional subtle warnings.

My sudden loss of energy would most often be during, or directly following, physical exertion. Even simple activities that I formerly did with ease such as climbing a staircase or going out to get more wood for the woodstove could cause me to feel like collapsing.

"I can't. " I would often catch myself complaining to friends.

Although I knew that my increasing insomnia was sometimes a contributing factor, it seemed that on most days the fatigue hit unexpectedly. In addition, the overwhelming tiredness was often combined with weepiness.

I remember several examples of my struggle with this common symptom of depression – times when Fatigued Francine nearly got the best of me.

***

My husband and I were upstairs one winter evening in a drafty old farmhouse. He was playing computer games, and I had collapsed on a mattress on the floor behind him, sobbing uncontrollably during one of my Weepy Wanda episodes and shivering in the cold room. After what felt like an eternity (but was probably only about 20 minutes), I had recovered enough from the wave of inner darkness to speak.

"I'm so cold!" I cried, nearly hysterical, pulling my sweater closer around me and trying to poke my frigid feet under the lightweight sheet on the mattress. When my husband did not respond, I repeated through my tears in a voice hardly above a whisper, "I'm cold!"

Without turning from his all-consuming computer game, irritated that I had dared to disturb him, he snapped at me, "Why don't you get yourself a blanket then?"

"I can't get up."

I couldn't even find the energy to go to the next room to get a blanket for myself, regardless of the fact that I was so cold that my teeth were chattering.

About 15 minutes later, again calling upon every last ounce of energy in my fatigued body and brain, I managed to start inching my way closer to the little space heater that was running near my husband's feet.

Though warmed by the device, how I longed for my man's *touch*! It would have been so comforting just to feel his hand on my shoulder, to revel in a moment of contact and connection with a live human being when I felt like a cold corpse.

As one writer describes her depression, "I curled up like a frozen prawn. Although I was not cold objectively, I acted as though I was desperately trying to conserve my body heat.... The only thing that gave me comfort was the feel of his hand on my back."[2]

***

Another time that Fatigued Francine showed up, I was helping my husband to load some tools and construction materials into his work van. I felt tired and had slowed down to the point where I was barely moving. Suddenly, I stopped dead in my tracks, unable to move at all.

My husband noticed and asked, "What's wrong?"

I burst into tears and replied in a nearly inaudible voice, "I'm so tired. I can't move!" I was literally rooted to the spot where I was standing. I couldn't put one foot in front of the other. I was paralyzed. This terrified me beyond words.

---

[2] Lewis, Gwyneth. *Sunbathing in the Rain.* New York: Flamingo, Harper Collins, 2003, p. 19.

"Come on," he insisted, "there are only a few more boxes to go."

I started sobbing. I literally could not move. I stood there like a statue, weeping uncontrollably and feeling very stupid. He went about his business while I stood with my face in my hands, trying to hide my humiliation at yet another meltdown.

A few minutes later when the van was all loaded up, he asked nonchalantly, "Do you still want to go to town with me?"

Under the circumstances, that seemed like a pointless question with an obvious answer. I shook my head and whispered disappointedly, "No, I can't go."

I stayed home and was eventually able to make it up the stairs to the bedroom where I collapsed onto the bed, sobbing my heart out and calling myself names for 'fizzling out' when my husband needed help. I felt so horrible for letting him down.

***

Fatigued Francine came another time after I was separated from my husband and sharing a large house with some friends. Early one morning, I had already gone for a short jog around the block and had cooked a pot of hot oatmeal for the others when Weepy Wanda made one of her unannounced appearances. I fled to my room for a sobbing session. I heard the others go into the kitchen and eat, wash their dishes, and leave for work; but I was still crying uncontrollably in the bedroom, getting hungrier by the minute.

Eventually, I heard one of my friends return to the kitchen so, trying to sound as natural as possible, I called out, "Are you there?" The door to my room popped open and in poked a head.

"What's up?" he asked, obviously in a hurry.

I was still curled up on the bed, powerless to sit up. "I'm hungry," I whispered between sobs.

"Why don't you get yourself some breakfast?" came the terse reply. "There's still some oatmeal in the pot. We're all finished."

"I can't!" I wailed. "I have no energy!"

Soon a bowl of steaming oatmeal was plunked down beside me on the bed.

"Now don't get used to being served breakfast in bed," he remarked, half in jest. Then he left rather abruptly, his mind and attention elsewhere.

On a normal day, I would have rolled my eyes at his comment, laughed together with him, and made a witty reply. But Fatigued Francine convinced me that I was a lazy lump, so I cried even harder, my rumbling stomach and hunger forgotten for the moment. I felt utterly incompetent, inadequate, and defective.

***

A few weeks later, I was trying to get some much-needed exercise by walking down the quiet country road one glorious spring day. After about 10 minutes of walking at a moderate speed, I had to slow to a snail's pace.

"I don't feel well," I thought to myself. "I'm so tired." Suddenly I stopped altogether, unable to put one foot in front of the other. I remembered my experience in the garage some years before. Again, I was terrified at being unable to move.

"What if I can't get back to the house?" I worried, even though I was little more than half a mile away. In addition to my body, my brain was in 'dead gear' also. But somehow, thank God, I was able to rationalize, "If I rest for a while, I might be able to get back, or maybe a neighbor will see me sitting on the side of the road and offer me a ride home."

Mortified, I looked around to see if anyone was watching. Of course, no one was even remotely close since most of my neighbors were at work. Besides, who cares whether a woman is sitting along a quiet country road? I sank to the ground, utterly exhausted. I felt so weak that I even considered lying completely flat on the ground but decided against it for fear that the neighborhood coyotes might be craving a soft, sweet bite of lunch. I rested on the side of the road for about 15 minutes until I felt strong enough to walk home unaided.

***

Recently, I discovered an entry from my prayer journal during that time. In it, I was addressing the Eternal God and expressing my battle with this extreme fatigue:

Convert me, Father, or better yet, just kill me before I hurt someone else or myself again. I do not have the strength to strive to follow You anymore – I am just too tired to work out my salvation. I am too tired to perform the duties You've given me. I don't even have the energy to be temperate anymore. Help me!

Harmful Hannah

The first time I hit myself on the head, I thought I had lost my mind. I do not remember how old I was, probably a teenager. It was in response to a painful situation with which I couldn't cope. However, I felt so much calmer after hitting myself that I decided it was not such a bad thing. Feeling the *physical* pain from the hits helped to release some of my *emotional* pain, and I felt more in control of overwhelming, uncontrollable situations.

That was then; this is now, and now I know better. The truth is that I have hurt myself far too much. The injuries have been severe enough to scare me – bruises, welts, headaches, possibly minor concussions. In God's mercy, He made me thick-skulled!

Thankfully, only a few people have observed me hitting myself or the results of it. Of those few, two reacted with natural alarm, "What are you doing? You're crazy!" – further evidence that I might actually *be* crazy.

The following incidents are included simply as representative samples of self-harm in my situation at the time. I would rather forget the overwhelming pain I experienced at the time of numerous similar incidents.

I wrote this journal entry five months into my second marriage:

Yes, the computer is more important than me or anyone else in your pitiful life, Stan. You are sick. You are addicted, whether you want to admit it or not. What person expects his new wife to wait an hour for a response to a simple yes or no question just because he is playing a computer game and is not at the end of a session? You do not care about our marriage or me. You're too focused on yourself and what you're doing to care. I am a fool to love a man who is only capable of loving himself. But I still love you, Stan.

I want to be invisible. I want to escape, to go far away from this man who cannot love. I want a loving, caring, affectionate, touching, warm, sensitive, listening man – the man I thought I married. What would happen if all I did were eat, sleep, and play computer games and did not work to support you, Stan?

I know that the Eternal One has given me faith to question Him, to seek solutions. I know that pouring out my heart to Him, as David, Job, and the Messiah himself did, does not come from weak faith as Stan asserts, but in knowing the Eternal well enough to be secure in the knowledge that He will not annihilate me for questioning Him but will come through for me, in His time and in His way, as He always does.

May I have space away from the man whose illness is driving me insane! I want to get away, far away, from him. I am starving. He gives me nothing; he has nothing to give. He has abandoned me. He has abandoned himself. He has abandoned God.

Father God, save me from this pain before I resort to hitting myself again. I feel so awful, so alone. I cry out to you with all my heart, Yahweh!

***

I recorded the following two self-harm incidents, just days apart, after I had already decided that it was time to leave this dead relationship:

My heart is aching. I hurt myself again. Stan promised not to play computer games anymore and deleted the ones on his computer. A few hours later, he downloaded a new one, and I am mourning. We will never be truly married as long as the 'other woman' is in his life. He only wants a cook and a housekeeper. That's all I'm good for. I am sad for his sake and for what he is missing in life and in love.

Oh, Eternal God, be my Husband and my happiness! I am alone again, discarded for a computer game.

Living on my own a short time later, I wrote:

Feeling very poorly about myself right now. Spent hours trying to set up internet in my new apartment and lost my temper while on hold with the phone company for the sixth time (literally). I started hurting myself again. I feel awful. I have no money. Do I ask Stan for some or go live on the streets? It hurts being in this position.

Weepy Wanda

Wanda was my most frequent and dreaded visitor. I will not call her a friend because, unlike a true friend, she would show up anytime, anywhere, unannounced and unwelcome. She virtually took over my life.

Sometimes I'd cry so hard that I'd hyperventilate or see stars and bursts of light. I often felt like I was going to pass out (though I was usually already lying on the floor, so I did not have far to go).

"Help me!" was the cry of my heart to no one in particular. "Touch me! Am I still alive? I feel so dead." Sometimes I would bury my face in my cat's fur and cry there just to touch a warm, living, breathing creature. I needed to feel her little chest rise and fall with each breath as I gently rested my head on her side. Sneezing into her fur (sorry, kitty!) reminded me that I was *alive*. Knowing that I had not killed myself brought the comfort I needed to finally catch a glimpse of the light beyond the shadows and eventually drag myself back to the real world.

"Not again!" I would groan inwardly when Wanda's weepy tears began to flow – usually spontaneous waves of sobbing; other times those weepy hours seemed to be triggered by someone or something. And I never knew if a weeping episode would last one hour, one day, or one week. Thankfully, Wanda usually retreated at night so I could get some sleep, only to start crying again the next morning . . . and the next.

Wanda was such a common visitor that I struggle to choose just a few weepy episodes to describe. The first one that usually comes to mind happened not so many years ago. I was mowing the lawn when suddenly I was overcome with tears, not just a tear or two, or a trickle, but the floodgates were opened. I was crying so hard that I couldn't see where

I was going, so I stopped the mower and stood quietly for a few moments, hoping it would pass. But Weepy Wanda did not leave; I kept crying. I looked around to see if my elderly neighbor was in her garden observing my odd behavior.

"No, she is inside." I breathed a prayer of gratitude. Then I sank to the ground and wept uncontrollably for about 20 minutes. Wanda won the battle. Defeated, I crawled into the house (literally), slowly making my way upstairs to hibernate in my room. The grass cutting had to wait until the next day.

When I later told a friend what had happened, she asked, "What were you crying about?"

"Nothing," I answered truthfully.

"Oh, surely you were thinking about something or someone, a painful memory perhaps," knowing that I had been amply supplied with such memories.

"No," I replied emphatically. "I was focusing on keeping my self-propelled mower in the right place and was not thinking about anything at all, much less something sad."

My friend shook her head skeptically thinking, like my mother years earlier, that people do not cry without a reason. A person who has not suffered from such attacks can rarely identify with such a predicament, hence the isolating nature of this disorder.

Another incident happened when I was getting to know my friend Lucas. We often spent time away from his house in the city at his country house, planting a garden, stacking firewood for the winter, and other pleasant chores. One Sunday morning, Lucas met Weepy Wanda for the first time. My journal entry at the end of the day, was as follows:

Dear Father God, this evening I praise You for Your goodness in teaming me up with Lucas at this specific point in my life. Today You loved me through him when he cooked breakfast for me and served me because I was weepy all morning and did not have the energy to get off the couch. That is a 'first' for me, and I felt truly loved, like the princess I am in You. Thank You for that wonderful gift, to know You can love me even when I have nothing to give in return. And thank you for letting Weepy Wanda leave by noon.

* * *

At another time, I had been on the verge of crying all day and finally decided to go to the public library to see if some intellectual stimulation and a change of scenery would help me avoid what prior experience told me was inevitable. An hour later, I was crying uncontrollably in the library, too ashamed to leave the building and walk home; I was stuck – a prisoner in the vegan cookbook section.

Much to my surprise, as I was stooping on the floor pretending to read a book, through my brain fog I heard someone call my name.

With great difficulty, Fatigued Francine, Weepy Wanda, and I stood up. There stood Lucas, who knew that Weepy Wanda was visiting. He had come to take me home. Even with him walking beside me on the way out to the car, I was self-conscious about my tear-stained face and swollen eyes. What would people think? But somehow I got out of the library, grateful for the rescue and thankful to soon be at home crying on my own bed.

***

When friends were invited over one Friday evening for a special meal and a Bible study, Wanda invited herself. I spent the entire afternoon helping Lucas prepare food for our friends. By the time the guests arrived, I had collapsed in tears and exhaustion in another room, leaving my housemates to conduct the gathering.

I had been looking forward to the evening all week. I wanted so much to enjoy the companionship of my friends. Alas, it was not to be, at least for Weepy Wanda and me.

***

Wanda appeared again when my sister's friend and her husband had taken us to their cottage on the lake. We had prepared a simple picnic lunch to share together. As we drove along, I noticed I was becoming more and more withdrawn. My energy was almost rock bottom. My speech was sluggish; and when I *did* speak, my voice was barely audible. I was unresponsive when they tried to include me in the conversation. I was far, far away and only heard their voices far off in the distance. Sure enough, 'the grim weeper' began her sobbing spell. Talk about embarrassing!

GwynethLewis describes a similar feeling of social isolation this way: "...I have found great comfort in listening to the radio in bed, sleeping through the chat of human voices, as

23

if I were a baby in the womb – within reach of conversation but not required to take part in it."[3]

I laid down on the backseat of the car in the parking lot, covered my head with a towel in shame, and wept for the next two hours. My sister and her friend fixed a lovely plate of delightful picnic goodies for me and placed it on the front seat of the car, but I was crying too hard to eat.

Eventually we all went home. I had cried through the entire picnic.

Irritable Iris and Raging Rhonda

Between bouts of fatigue and lethargy, I often become cranky and downright red-hot angry. I tend to pick fights and do some button-pushing on anyone I find irritating or stupid. Irritability and rage are perhaps the most feared of all my symptoms because I do not trust myself as to what I might do when these three are present, whether individually or collectively.

The following is a journal entry:

Didn't sleep well last night. Had a dream in which I was going around saying, "I hate myself" to others and to myself. I woke up with clenched fists. I feel stuck in my anger and do not know what to do with it. Intellectually, I know it's not good, but the feelings are still there.

---

[3] Lewis, 26.

One evening, when a friend and I were staying in a short-term rental and trying to edit his book, he stepped out for a while. He promised to come back soon.

When bedtime came and he still had not returned, I began to worry. I had not gotten much sleep the night before (typical of the insomnia that often accompanies PMDD) and did not want a repeat performance. I was extremely tired. Soon I started stewing over the situation. I figured he was probably just down at the pool listening to songs on YouTube.

"I am going to go out there and give him a piece of my mind," I grumbled to myself. I stomped down the stony path toward the pool with both barrels loaded.

Sure enough, he was sitting there, coolly watching something on YouTube. I lost it and gave him a brief but volatile tongue-lashing.

"I was just finishing up!" he defended himself indignantly.

Not wanting to go back to the house alone in the dark, I sat my self-righteous self near the pool in the dark to wait for him to finish, continuing to 'chew him out' in my mind.

About 10 minutes later, I returned to the Wi-Fi area to see if he was done. But he was nowhere in sight. He had gone back to the house by himself without saying a word to me! He had taken the flashlight and left me in the dark!

Of course, then I was more furious than ever. I stormed back to the house, preparing to give him another tongue-lashing.

"Is he thoughtless or what?" I screamed to myself. I was so overtired by that point that I was not thinking straight; I could only see red. I started up the hill, crying at being left alone in the dark, feeling abandoned. As this was in a tropical country, I was deathly afraid of the poisonous snakes that had been spotted along that section of the road.

About halfway up to the house, knowing he couldn't be but a few minutes ahead of me on the road, I started calling his name. No response.

"Where in the world *is* he?" I wondered. I knew my voice was loud enough to carry up the hill in the silence of the night (and for the other guests to hear).

"Why doesn't he respond?" Before long, frantic and furious, I was screaming his name at the top of my lungs. There was still no response. When I got up to the house, there was Mr. Arrogant standing at the door.

"Why are you yelling?" he asked nonchalantly. "I could hear you all the way down the hill." He was calm and comfortable, the little turkey.

"Then why didn't you come and help me?" I cried hysterically. To lay some guilt on him, I blurted out a fabricated story about seeing a huge poisonous snake. Then I dropped, exhausted, onto the bed, weeping uncontrollably, anger forgotten.

Did he have any words of comfort for poor me, terrified and hysterical? None whatsoever. Instead, he grabbed his camera and went to look for the snake! I could hardly believe it. No compassion, no concern for me.

"You jerk!" I screamed at him as he went out the front door.
"I hope it bites you!"

He started laughing and asked, "Why are you so upset
about seeing a snake?"

At that moment, I was too consumed with hatred to reply.
I laid there and cried alone until midnight when I finally fell
asleep from sheer exhaustion.

All Symptoms Simultaneously

This journal entry was written three months into my
marriage to Stan. It has PMDD written all over it, although I
did not recognize the symptoms at the time:

*It's morning, I guess, but dark outside as usual and even
darker in my heart. I am crying again. So tired of crying. Sick
of feeling like this – dragging myself around with no hope
that today will be any different from yesterday. I want to
put all the cat condo materials away; he will never build that
thing. I am so angry and tired of staring at the stuff, tired of
the clutter in this tiny apartment. I don't have the energy to
play with the cats these days. I don't even feel like
showering or getting dressed – no one sees me, and Stan
could care less what I look like. I don't want to do anything
– it takes too much energy just to do the necessary stuff, so
I do not even exercise these days. I am tired of crying myself
to sleep simply because I am so exhausted and cold and
lonely. Every day is just more of the same. Every day, I sink
a little lower, and the darkness gets a bit denser. Every day,
my dreams get more distant, my hope decreases. Every day
is forever dark.*

The next incident happened during one of those dark days in Central America when I did not think I would make it through to the other side because I was experiencing all symptoms simultaneously.

I was camping near my friend's house on the river. My friends were at another house about a mile down the road sharing a Bible study, fellowship, and guitar music, and I was stuck in 'the rubber room' (my tent) with Wanda. It was just not fair! Although it had been raining all day, someone delivered bananas and other food to me and Weepy Wanda in the tent.

When a tropical downpour began, I was very thankful that I had tied a tarp over the tent earlier that day. I was more or less dry until one enormous torrent of rain. It was as if someone had dumped several thousand buckets of water over my tarp. The nylon tent began to leak, so I started mopping up water with clothes from my laundry pile.

"Boy, it's really coming down!" I remember thinking to myself. It was well past my bedtime, and I was exhausted from crying all day, so I attempted to go to sleep.

Suddenly I heard a loud sound in the distance, a cross between a roar and a rumble, getting louder and louder as the minutes passed. I knew it was not the roar of an animal. A minute or two later, I sat bolt upright, unable to ignore the sound any longer. Could it be the river?

I yanked the tent flap open and stuck my head out into the darkness, only to discover that, within a matter of minutes, the river down from my tent had risen to twice its usual height and was thundering past my tent without any thought of stopping. My quiet river was suddenly a raging flood!

I watched in horror for the next 10 minutes as the water continued to rise. Recognizing the dangerous situation I was in, I panicked and thought, "What if the water continues to rise?" I immediately started carrying my stuff through the dark downpour to a dry, covered area beside the house. Eventually I got everything relocated and just left the empty tent down by the raging river.

In reality, I was in no immediate danger of the water sweeping me away because, even by morning, the water had not crested and was still feet away from the tent. But the power of that water thundering past the tent and rising so rapidly was enough to trigger my terror. At the same time, I was thankful I had not fallen asleep and then been woken up by the raging floodwaters!

Out of immediate danger, I started crying again and said to myself, "There's no way I am going to sleep alone now!"

Then I did the unthinkable – in my panicky confusion, I got dressed and headed down the road into the pitch-black night, my tiny folding umbrella useless against the driving rain. I did not know where I was going, and I did not care how long it took me to get there.

Soaked, terrified, and still sobbing, I experienced the walk of a lifetime. The road was one enormous mud puddle, almost a pond in some places. With no flashlight, I could hardly stay on the muddy road in my slippery flipflops. I thought of poisonous snakes and frogs in the deep puddles yet determinedly kept plodding on, slip sliding down the hill, praying that I would end up at my friends' house alive. At least there was a method in my madness.

At one point, the road was so dark that I started singing just to ease my anxiety. I confess I had an overwhelming urge to lay down in the mud to await the outcome.

Sobbing, singing, and sliding, I eventually made it to my friends' house, soaked and terrified. I was too embarrassed for them to see me in that condition, so I waited in the rain some distance from the house until one of them noticed me from the protected patio area. He came under the umbrella where I stood dripping and trembling, by then almost hysterical with fear.

"The river is rising!" I blurted out. He quickly explained the situation to our hosts who tactfully said goodnight from a distance, and my friend drove me back to his house.

On the way, crying harder than ever, I confessed almost inaudibly, "When I saw the rising floodwaters, all I could think about was how easy it would be to throw myself in there." That was my most concrete suicide 'plan' in years, and I was terrified that I might go through with it unless someone was around to ground me in reality. Once again, I felt like I was on the edge of insanity.

My friend helped me out of the truck and into the house. With great effort, I changed into some dry clothes and fell exhausted onto the bed where I cried myself to sleep.

When I reflect (not very often!) on that frightening experience, I remember that I did not recognize the 'person' who wanted to plunge into that raging river. Whose voice was I hearing in my mind? Where was it coming from? And since I did not recognize that voice or that 'person' in my body, how could I know what she was capable of doing? All I know is that her voice was louder than my own at that moment.

From that terrifying night, I have learned that during the darkest periods of my life, it's wise to stay away from the edge of subway platforms, the windows of tall buildings, and the banks of raging rivers because I cannot trust the stranger in my body.

"Save me, God,
for the waters have come up to my neck!
I sink in deep mire, where there is no foothold.
I have come into deep waters,
where the floods overflow me.
I am weary with my crying.
My throat is dry.
My eyes fail looking for my God."

Psalm 69:1-3

Chapter 3 – On the Edge of Insanity

Pushing Myself to the Max

After tracking my cycle and moods, I gradually became aware that the duration of the 'low' phases was increasing each month. Some of these phases were so long that I was barely out of one three-week low when the next one would hit a week later. I also noticed that my lows were intensifying, meaning that I was experiencing more days with suicidal thoughts and self-harm. In addition, as my menstrual cycle became irregular due to perimenopause, my formerly predictable misery became unpredictable, erratic surprises. I could no longer plan more than an hour or two in advance because I never knew what condition I would find myself in by the next week, the next day, or even the next hour.

Regular employment was impossible because, in addition to the unpredictable, uncontrollable crying and rage, I also struggled with severe insomnia and chronic fatigue. The best I could do was work as a housekeeper in exchange for room and board.

"I have got to keep doing as much as I can," I told myself, knowing that people were depending on me. I pushed myself to the maximum to keep functioning as normally as possible, although I could scarcely drag myself out of bed most mornings. I often thought, "When can I just curl up and die? Why should I continue existing in misery like this? I have nothing to live for."

As hard as I tried, I just couldn't come up with a reason to hang on. Consequently, when I found myself locked in the dark dungeon of depression, more and more frequently I could see no way out, no light, no hope – and suicide looked like the only way to end my agony.

While experiencing a lot of 'down days' in the summer of 2011, I asked some friends if I could stay alone for several weeks at their little camp property. I desperately wanted to be alone, as far away from people as I could get since, for me, people equaled stress. I also wanted to be able to get up late if I needed to because of my insomnia, or sleep all day for that matter, with no responsibility for anyone else, no obligation to make anyone's breakfast, wash their clothes, or clean up after them. I wanted to be responsible only for myself for a change. But at that point, I was not even sure if I could take care of *me*. Fatigued Francine was my constant companion.

My plan to camp in solitude and to take care of myself failed. Although I camped alone for several weeks, I was in a deep, dark, intense depression the entire time, the worst up to that point if my memory serves me correctly. Yes, I enjoyed being by myself and not needing to cook meals for anyone, having time to go for long walks in the woods if I had the energy, and being in charge of my own schedule. However, I ended up being *completely* isolated with no telephone, no electricity for my laptop, and no internet. There was no possibility of communication with anyone. I nearly took my own life several times.

I did not want to return to the house in the city because the situation was far too stressful there, and the noisy nights increased my insomnia. However, I was terrified of what I might do to myself if I remained alone at the camp. As a result, I wrote to my sister, "Can you come and stay with me for a couple of weeks?"

She unquestioningly responded to my appeal for help and immediately booked a flight. By the time she arrived, however, I was already in the upswing of the cycle, and we simply enjoyed our time together. Perhaps my sister's company brought a degree of security and comfort that lowered my anxiety level, and my body was able to cope better. For whatever reason, I felt much better and remained unusually high functioning.

My sister invited me to stay with her in the city, which I did, sleeping on the floor but thankful for food and shelter and a semblance of sanity. That phase of relative normalcy lasted through September and October, although I still had occasional low days, as seen in this journal entry:

Not feeling good this morning. Dizzy, heavy-headed, and under a cloud. Thoughts are rambling.

I feel like I am not being true to myself still, although I know I do not have too many options at this point. I am here in the city again, hearing all the traffic and sirens, the masses of people everywhere that I cannot get away from. There is no access to grass or anything fresh from the soil, or my own patch of trees to look at, or fresh air to breathe.

I feel angry and irritated that I am stuck again just because of my 'issues.' When do I start living instead of worrying about where my next meal is coming from and what I have to do to keep people happy? I hate asking for anything, much less everything. I hate being dependent on others. I hate myself for being so irritable and disagreeable. I hate having to agree with people that I want to disagree with.

Journey to the Tropics

I decided at that point that perhaps a change of scenery would help me cope with the constant dark clouds in my life. Thus, in the fall of that year, I flew to Central America, joining a local family in a seaport town to do some health work using natural remedies in their community and to teach their children English.

The following are excerpts from several journal entries written at the beginning of the endeavor:

11/3/11 – I am on the next leg of my journey – out of the big city where I have been for the past two months.

How do I feel about being in a foreign country, living out of a suitcase again, not knowing how I am going to pay for my bananas? It's a scary situation. I have been here before.

I woke up with a bad headache again this morning, but I am thankful for this private hotel room with a little lamp on the table in the corner, a decent night's sleep, a quiet resting place, a window that opens to the air, birds chirping outside, and no rain at the moment. I am thankful for arms and legs that function.

The Sea Port

11/5/11 – I am finally at my destination. The 12-hour bus trip from the city to the seaport was a blast. Feeling a bit dizzy and have my usual headache.

Wayne was at the bus terminal to meet me, and together we hoisted my suitcases into the back of a truck to get them to the house. I slept on the bottom bamboo bunk in the kids' room last night.

The family had two surprises for me: Wayne had made a bed frame for me with purpleheart wood – a special tropical hardwood. The other surprise is that they have a cat, and she is pregnant!

It sure feels good to 'have a place to hang my hat.' We will see what works out for income. Right now, I just want to rest, rest, rest and do nothing for a while. I need the lowest stress job that a person can find, and yet I must remain financially independent somehow.

My Own Space

11/12/11 – It's so wonderful to have my own space now and a computer that functions. It's so easy to forget that I have a right to live on this planet as much as anyone else does; I deserve to be treated as a princess of the King of the Universe. I deserve some happiness in this life. May I honor Him with my life and serve Him with all my heart.

Work

11/15/11 – This morning, I spent an hour with the principal of the only international school for miles around; she showed me around the school compound and introduced me to the other teachers. In January, I will start teaching English twice a week. It felt great to be back 'on the school scene' even if it has been eight years since I have been in a classroom. And it feels great to have a teaching job again!

Hibernating Again

Although I felt fantastic for the first two weeks I was in Central America and was able to assist at two local health clinics, by the middle of the month, my mood had dipped again, and I mentally unraveled and plunged into despair, as seen in the following entry:

11/18/11 – Got my period today after a long and miserable day yesterday. Went for a long walk on the beach, 6.5 miles, but felt horrible the whole time. I had no energy; I was weepy, etc. I cried and hibernated the rest of the day. Today also, I have very low energy.

Desperate for Sleep

As the days passed and November turned into December, the suicidal thoughts were coming *every day*. I hated myself and everyone around me. As you read the dialogs between a friend and myself that follow later in this chapter, please keep in mind that depression affects a person's ability to reason from cause to effect, and my brain was definitely not processing properly. This is how I remember things, which may or may not be totally accurate:

12/13/11 – Midnight, in my tent. I just came back from walking on the beach with Maria's family, and I am still waiting for the others to return from their midnight fishing expedition.

I have failed again at living with others. I cannot do it with my disability. I cannot live with anybody. I need to live alone. If I kill myself living alone, then I kill myself. I must take the risk. Living other people's lifestyles is not the answer for me or for my health, at least at this point. I have been doing that all of my life.

If I ever get some sleep tonight and there is a tomorrow for me, I am going to take myself to the beach and stay all day, rain or shine. I have got to get out of this situation. I am not normal, and I do not function like a normal person.

Later – They are back from fishing and not even pretending to be quiet. It's 12:06 a.m. Such thoughtful people.... I feel like I could go insane from lack of sleep here.

So there I was, depressed again, tenting in the yard of a local family in Central America and desperately needing a place of my own. But how do you explain to 7- and 10-year-olds (the children in the family) that you are not crying because you're sad – that you're just crying because you cannot stop? How do you explain that you want to take them swimming but that you do not have enough energy to? How do you explain that your puffy eyes are not their problem? And how do you explain it all without speaking a word of Spanish?

After spending several weeks in my rainy tent, crying and with constant insomnia, a friend of mine arrived from North America. Together we found a quieter, more remote camping place, away from the chickens, dogs, and other night noises of the town.

After a week or two of camping there, we packed up and went to visit some friends in another town. That would have been fine and dandy, but Weepy Wanda was my 24/7 roommate again, and she and I were so tired of each other. Day after day, hour after hour, I cried and cried in my tent.

One day faded into the next and I hardly knew where I was, much less *who* I was, who I was with, or what I was saying and doing. I was oblivious to what was happening around me. Sometimes the crying would pass by the afternoon, but it always started again the next morning with renewed intensity.

Suicide again looked like the only option available to end my misery, my dark existence. People's voices were just noise to me. I couldn't see colors or hear music. Everything around me looked gray. Details went unobserved. I took no pleasure in seeing a sky full of stars or a brilliant sunrise. I did not care about anything or anyone, especially myself.

Finally, on December 20, I scribbled the following flow of woeful words on some scraps of paper in my tent, with Weepy Wanda and Harmful Hannah goading me on:

Forever Dark
Day…
or is it night?
I am blind.
It's dark, always dark.
"Look, the sun is shining," they say.
But I see only dense black clouds.
They lift for just a moment
or maybe even a few hours,
but they rush back
and settle on me like a soggy wool blanket,
smothering me, choking me.
I wrestle against the darkness.
It triumphs every time.
Father God, I want to see light.
Other people see light,

why can't I?
I need light, *Your* Light,
the light of Your Love.
I know You see me crying in the dark.
I know Your arms enfold me.
But I feel so alone, forsaken, forgotten,
inconsolable,
a solitary soul.
When will this darkness end?
Is it because of my faults and failures?
I only want to be alone
in a quiet place:
no dogs, chickens, babies,
children shouting in the street,
couples yelling in the houses,
music blaring from all sides,
early morning weed whackers grumbling,
blenders whirring, dishes clanging,
personalities clashing. . .
I can't take the noise anymore!
My feverish nerves have reached their limit.
The tiniest sound startles me.
Every noise engulfs me.
I cry and cry and cry.
There's no end to the tears.
I want to live again, to be happy,
to have something to hope for,
meaningful work to do,
meaningful friendships.
Instead, I get drained energy,
never-ending tears,
chronic stress.
Smile and say 'hello',
smile and say 'goodbye',

smile and say, 'thank you.'
I am sick of being polite!
Blah! Sick of it!
I am too dead to be polite,
too dead to even fake a smile,
too dead to conceal the tears
behind my mask anymore –
internally dead.
I wish I were dead on the outside too.
I feel so sick.
There's no end to this misery.
Over and over,
day in and day out.
Sobbing, weeping, crying, bawling,
I am nobody, a nonentity.
I do not belong.
There is no place in this world for me,
no safe corner of my own.
There is someone in my space,
but I smile and say, "It's ok."
It's too stressful to say
I need that space worse than he does.
I do not have the energy to say "no."
It takes less energy to acquiesce
than to disagree.
Eternal God, help me.
I cry out to You for relief
for You alone can save me.
Yahweh, rescue me!
"It's a beautiful day," they say.
"The sun is finally shining.
It's warm, the birds are happy."
Everybody is smiling.
"Why are you crying?"

Why *am* I crying?
What's wrong with me?
Father, end my life!
I hate myself for crying all the time.
I hate myself for being in constant pain
because I am always exhausted.
I hate people for expecting me
to 'snap out of it.'
I hate people for expecting me
to humiliate myself
by showing my swollen eyes
and tear-stained face in public.
I hate people promising to help
and then not visiting the prisoner
when she is in prison
and needs food and water.
I am angry –
at myself,
and people,
and yes, at You,
Eternal God.
You brought me into this world
but why to a painful existence like this?
Why can't I be happy like ordinary people?
Why do I have to be different, unusual?
Why depression?
Is it punishment for sins?
It's more than I can bear.
So dark, Dark, DARK!
You gave me life –
Please take it away.
I am exhausted,
tired of being miserable
and having to retreat

from the world to hide my misery.
Completely drained,
like I am 90 years old
and ready to lie down and die
instead of a youthful 47.
I give up!
Father, if You want me here,
breathe for me
and keep me alive
for Your glory.
My heart's desire is to die.
Do what you want with me.
You're the Creator
and I am just a speck
in Your vast creation.
Save me –
in my misery
and *from* my misery.
Then I can encourage others
in a similar plight.
And I know there *are* others,
countless women without hope,
just like I am.
Where is the joy You promised
comes in the morning?
I have begged for it again and again.
Divine Father, fill me with Your joy!
I feel left out of Your blessings.
I do not belong on this earth;
I am so different
and just want to be alone
in peace and quiet.
Eternal God, what do You want me to do?
What can I pray for besides death?

What can I do to get out of this dark world?
I will do anything!
I hate myself for being this way.
Who can help me?
Is this wretched existence
all I have to look forward to?
If it is, then take me off this planet.
I am numb, frozen,
except for the unrelenting ache
in my weary heart.
Nothing matters now,
only finding relief.
Where are You, Father God?
Where can I find healing for my brokenness,
my shattered life, the fragments of my heart,
a place of rest for my mind and body?
Where can I find true tranquility?
Yahweh, help me! Please!

Help!

Deep sigh. The silence of the week between December 20 and December 27 speaks eloquently of the corpse-like condition I was in. There was never a time in my life that I couldn't write anything on paper to express my thoughts and feelings – until that week of total darkness.

This was my final journal entry for the month, as well as for the year 2011, written on December 27:

I woke up with another night sweat. If it's not one thing waking me up, it's another. Then the attack of the itches (chigger bites). I am so itchy I feel like I could crawl out of my skin. No proper shower for days.

I am tired. That is nothing new. Exhausted. Nothing new. I cannot think of any other word that expresses the chronic fatigue I feel every day, even first thing in the morning.

I hate myself for being abnormal. I hate myself for wanting to be alone so much. Why can't I just fit in? I am at the end of my rope, and there is no knot at the bottom. What haven't I tried yet? Whether I am alone or with others, it's a lose-lose situation for me.

I am free – no children, no job, no husband – so why stay in Central American at all? I thought I could do it, but I am too ill. I will be in the emotional ICU as long as I live unless I make some decided changes. Should I stay here and try to use a drug like Prozac? What about checking into a mental health ward and getting them to drug me? Welcome relief from the pain! That sounds like a horribly desperate option, but that is how I feel about living right now – horribly desperate.

Hopeless

The next day was not much better for me. In fact, the situation seemed to go from "the worst" to "worse than the worst" as seen in the following entry:

Next day – 7:30 a.m. – Lucas and I just had our worst argument ever. This was no squabble. Why can't I just come out and tell him that I cannot live near him – that it's too stressful for me right now?

He stood in the house, insisting on telling me something he thought I needed to hear (his usual "you shouldn't have, you should have" lecture).

"Please stop," I said, already in tears and not ready for another hammer on my head after being awake all night and loathing myself the entire time.

He ignored my request, and his lecture tape seemed to play on for months and years.

"Please!" I finally said, raising my voice a notch, "respect what I am asking, and just stop."

But there was no stopping him. He was determined to say what he wanted to say.

That is when I made a critical mistake. Still in the doorway, I mustered all my courage, stood directly in front of him, and said in a no-nonsense voice, "Stop it!"

He shoved me out of the way. I lost my balance, falling first over the sofa and then onto the floor in a heap. All he did was keep shouting and swearing.

"Get out!" I cried hysterically (when I had recovered from the shock enough to pick myself up off the floor). "Get out!" He did not budge. Instead, he kept right on yelling at me! With almost superhuman strength, I was finally able to push the door shut on him, but not without a struggle. He was going to finish his speech. He walked all around the house, continuing to shout through the windows what I had done wrong.

"You're abusive!" I screamed back at him, for lack of a better word. He was livid. I fled into the bathroom, shut the door, and crouched on the floor. Still crying hysterically, I started

pounding on my head with my fists. My heart was broken, and I wanted to break my head too. I pounded away at my skull.

To make a long story short, he eventually reached the end of his lecture and turned on the usual sob story tape. I opened the door, and we shared a conciliatory hug. Oh, what a fool I am!

I am too sick for this. I am going deeper and deeper into the pit, and I am afraid I will not make it out of the hole one day.

He kept asking, "Are you going back to your sister's apartment in the city?" like I have no other options. He knows I am stuck, and he is glad.

***

The very next entry:

I just beat myself up again. These feelings of hatred, the self-loathing, the daily fixation with dying — it's getting worse and worse. I do not feel like eating. I do not feel like getting out of bed. I do not feel like talking to anyone, even small talk. I do not feel like walking or any other movement. I just long for an end to each day, an end to the misery and pain and darkness of this existence. I'm not me! I am someone else, an ugly stranger that I refuse to accept or love. She is crying out for help, and no one is listening.

Wave after wave of self-hatred keeps washing over me. I hate myself! I hate myself! I hate myself! I want to hurt, Hurt, HURT myself! Really hurt! Feel the pain, what deep intense pain...from where? God, help me! Save me from myself!

Do I want to remain unhealed or move on toward health and healing? I am leaving this country in January on my scheduled ticket.

What is supposed to carry me through black day after black day after black day? I am at the end of my rope. I cannot hang on. The neighbor's rock music is going again. My head is so sore. Here comes another wave of hatred. No hope. Black. Dark. Eternally.

***

Finally, I had lost my grip on the rope, and in desperation I begged Lucas, "Please take me to a pharmacy so I can buy a drug to help me! Please! I don't know what else to do!" I collapsed again into the seemingly endless sobbing. My world was totally black. There was no light.

Lucas did not need to beg. He was as ready as I was to throw in the towel and do anything to help me return to the land of the living. We drove to the nearest town, and I bought some Prozac (a common antidepressant) over the counter. What did I have to lose? Morphing into a weepy, wall-staring, man-hating, death-craving robot for up to two weeks out of every month was equally bad or worse than the risk of the side effects of an antidepressant. Using a drug was the only way I knew to stay in the battle, and I had to give life one last attempt.

I knew the drug was not the ultimate solution for my depression or a 'cure' for it, but I did not care at that point.

I was desperate for relief – something, *anything*, just to keep me alive long enough to find more permanent relief.

"Let nothing disturb thee, nothing affright thee.
All things are passing, God never changes.
Patient endurance attaineth to all things.
Who God possesses, in nothing is wanting.
Alone God suffices."

St. Theresa of Avila

Chapter 4 – He Gave Me Wings to Fly

Making My Move

Three days later, I was out of danger and within a week, I was out of the dungeon. After all those weeks of crying, I felt like a new person. I smiled occasionally, even laughed sometimes. The drug returned me to reality long enough for me to receive a new opportunity for recovery and joyous living.

Longing for a Healing Place

Once the medication kicked in, I could see more clearly what I needed to do and where I needed to be to continue the upward climb toward healing. Even so, I did not act, as can be observed in the following journal excerpts:

1/5/12 – It seems that every morning when I wake up in this tent at Tim's place again, I hear a voice telling me that I am in the wrong environment for healing. I have been on Prozac for a week now. I am not waking up crying which is a blessed relief, but I am still discouraged about not having a place to call home, somewhere to unpack my bags for more than a week at a time, and to get a routine going. I do not know when my next meal will be because of all the people and commotion in the kitchen and what food is available. It seems unending. I finally have a quiet corner in nature where I can sleep when I want and wake up naturally, but the rest of the healing environment is not available. I must do something to get out of this rut.

I am not going back to the almost catatonic condition that I was in last week. No way, no how. I would rather be dead than nearly comatose! It was less than existing because there was no quality of life at all. Who can understand the desperation of that statement except someone who has suffered as much as I have for as long as I have? I need to stop living the life other people think I should be living.

Years have passed since I have been in a stable environment. The closest I came was probably when I was with my second husband. Our house was in a rural area, we had a big garden, and there was plenty of sunshine. Losing that healing environment because of his gaming addiction was a true catastrophe for me.

My inner voice says that I will heal more if I am away from emotional vampires. It hurts to say that but inside, I know it's true. Eternal God, please make a way for me to get away from Lucas.

Truth Requires Energy

1/6/12, 4 a.m. – Yesterday I told Lucas I will leave Central America at the end of the month.

He asked excitedly, "When's your flight?" In the next breath, he said, "What will it take to keep you here?"

Why do I feel like there is no healing in Lucas' presence? I find myself searching for excuses just to get away from him. Is it because I always need to explain and defend myself instead of trusting my own reasoning? Being true to myself takes a lot of energy.

1/11/12 – I feel like a slave. Lucas had another angry outburst today. I know what I need to do now. The decision has finally been made, the same decision I made nearly a year ago but did not follow up on. It's time to cut the cord.

I said calmly, quietly, "I feel like a slave when I am around you because when I say 'no,' you get angry and defensive or try to talk me into your way of seeing things. Or you have a pity party."

He was still trying to grasp what I was saying, so I calmly continued, "I know that you know that I have nowhere to go. I feel like I am stuck. I have to do what you want."

He got defensive, claiming how good he is and how compassionate and how much he has put up with and how hard he is trying and that he was going to drive to the market to get me anything I wanted, and then he started telling me how hungry he was and how he had not eaten all day… Then he switched gears and stormed off between expletives saying, "Go on welfare! Go to your sister's! You've had bags under your eyes since you went on the drug. You're on your own!"

I feel broken. Spent. Used. Sick. Exhausted. Homeless. I have nothing except the will to keep fighting, which is more than I had a week ago. This in itself is a miracle, a gift from the Most High, and I am grateful.

***

Knowing Lucas the way I did, I knew he was not finished with the topic of my departure. I knew he would be back. And just as I predicted, he came back, and we had the following exchange:

"What can I do to help you?" he asked sweetly.

(Help me? How about listening for a change?)

He stayed at my tent, being all nice and chummy and defending himself and correcting me. He kept going on and on about the devil trying to break apart our friendship.

When he paused to take a breath, I finally said, "Please stop. I will come up to your tent when I am ready to talk."

He started to continue his lecture, so I repeated, "I am asking you nicely, Lucas, please stop. You deserve my full attention because what you have to say is important, but my mind just is not in a place to listen yet." (That was a pretty bold thing for me to say!)

He stormed out of the room.

I have such a headache.

"You're my best friend and I love you," he had told me earlier. Is this what love looks like — guilt heaped on me when I say no? Barking orders at me? Expecting me to do things that I do not even have the strength to do?

Later, he said something that sounded like an apology. He was very docile, of course, as if I have nothing to be scared of. He keeps saying, "I will be all alone if you leave now. I'd rather you be around and sick than not around at all." It used to sound believable, but now it seems hollow when he says it. This rollercoaster drives me nuts.

1:38 a.m. – What a headache! And clenched, tired, aching jaws. Nevertheless, I love to hear the creek dribbling by, the frogs, and the crickets. I'd miss that if I lived somewhere else, also sleeping out in the open air.

All I know is that I dread going down to his tent in the mornings for water or passing by to get out to the road for a walk, knowing he is going to complain about something. He is constantly asking me to do something that I do not want to do or cannot do. Who wants to be around a person like that? I have to say 'yes' or fear the backlash.

3:26 a.m. – Headache still bad. Migraine. Seeing stars. Ate a banana and took a Prozac pill (since it often makes me sleepy). I feel so drained. There are no happy or healing options, so I feel blocked on every side. My goal is to preserve every shred of self-respect and health that I have remaining and focus on healing: soul, mind, and body. How can I heal around toxic people when I do not have the energy to stand up for myself?

***

My gloomy mind struggled to remember a time when life with Lucas was not so toxic to me. To his credit, there were indeed many instances that came to mind – times when he was a real pleasure to be around, and times when I sensed his care for me was genuine.

One such time was when he offered to take me to the beach so I could unwind and get some much-needed sunshine and fresh air while he ran some errands. When he came to pick me up and could not find the exact spot where he had dropped me off, he drove around frantically looking for me.

When we finally reconnected a couple hours later, his obvious concern for my wellbeing warmed my heart. We then spent some time together enjoying the waves. Ah, if only *every* moment together could have been like that afternoon beside the ocean.

Excerpt from an Email to My Sister

Eventually, by the grace of God, I made the all-important decision to leave Central America. With Prozac still surging through my system, I had enough clarity of mind to act on that decision. I knew what I had to do. I wrote the following email to my sister:

1/12/12 – Dear Sis, I am not staying. I have a few vague thoughts of what to do next. I cannot take stress right now, just don't have the strength to deal with anything or anyone. Not that I can eliminate all stress from my life – that is unrealistic – but some stress you can just anticipate.

Making this move is so hard, but I believe it will be a step forward to healing. Healthy relationships are part of my healing, just as unhealthy ones are part of the cause of the pain, and I do not have many healthy relationships now.

As far as praying about it goes, well, I have been crying out for an answer. This morning, I read a few pages in a book where the author counseled a couple that if the woman agreed to stay in that particular situation, she was going to lose her womanhood and wear out her life and get discouraged, unfitting her for the Lord's service. And I feel like that is what is happening here because I have no energy. I am losing my personhood. It's time to let go of Lucas.

It's All My Fault (As Usual)

Of course, the stressful part was sharing my decision with Lucas:

1/14/12, 12:44 a.m. – Told Lucas my decision yesterday. As expected, he was neither surprised nor happy when he dug for reasons. He probably received mixed messages, though, because I tried to come up with reasons to leave Central America that did not involve him. But eventually, perhaps because he knew already, he probed long enough and dug deep enough for me to connect the leaving with him.

Here are some of the arguments he tried:

- *You do not accept me as I am;*
- *Nobody else has a problem with my raising my voice (therefore, your statement is not valid);*
- *I have never had to raise my voice with other people (therefore, you are the problem, you made me do it);*
- *Your illness makes you very sensitive (therefore, you make mountains out of a molehills – things that are no big deal to 'normal' people);*
- *You have nowhere to go (therefore, you need me);*
- *I will try harder (for how long? I have heard that so many times it's sickening);*
- *It's my mother's fault (he started telling stories about how he was abused as a child).*

I am proud to say that I did not fall for any of it, as can be seen in the following entry:

By evening, he was all sweet and charming, and I read a few pages of an inspirational book to him. Lucas knows he has economic control over me right now and is offering to pay me to work for him. But he would still be the boss, and I need to be free to be me. Any tie with him at this point is simply too complicated.

When was the last time he asked about my dreams and goals, my desires, my needs? Is this because he expects them to be the same as his? Or because he is always right?

My suitcase is packed, and I am ready to go, but I have two more stressful weeks to endure. Why does it take me so long to extricate myself from bad relationships? I have known about this for almost a year. Yes, I am sick, but so sick that I need to be dependent? Nope. I would rather die first, and I may. It's ok – I am ready. At least I will die being me.

Energy!

1/16/12 – Feeling lots of energy yesterday and today and have not done anything different than in previous days. I even ran a few steps last evening.... Feels good to have a bit of energy instead of being so draggy and slow motion, like a sloth. May it's because I finally made a decision that I know is right?

***

Still Searching for Peace

Facing the results of my announcement was even more distressing than I had anticipated, but I stuck with my decision:

1/19/12 – Lucas asked again, "What are you going to have somewhere else that I am not providing?"

"Peace," I answered.

I think my answer blew him away. I know it blew me away!

I explained the best I could about the energy it takes to interact with people in close relationships. He did not blow his top, but I could tell he was on the brink. The volcano was definitely smoldering.

"You're a strange bird," he told me.

"I think I am very normal," I replied. "I just want to feel safe and be heard."

He said nothing.

***

Lucas went for a walk with me this evening. Sounded a bit repentant; but I know from experience that it just does not last. He'll blow again. He'll gripe again. He'll manipulate again. He'll blame me again. He'll hoodwink me again. I am leaving in a week. That sounds strange when I have nowhere to go. It feels strange not to be getting ready for the flight back to the U.S. What am I hoping for, a miracle? 1/22/12, 1:52 a.m. Lucas was as sweet as could be yesterday: loving, kind, gentle, thoughtful, making me smile, complimenting me, treating me like a queen, etc. But how many days can he persevere?

Ants and Urine

The stress of facing the music was wearing on me. Little things that would not have bothered me under different circumstances became mountains of difficulty:

1/22/12 – I am so discouraged. Sitting here in a stinky tent and cannot sleep. No supper except a few bananas (although they were exceptionally tasty). I knocked over my pee bucket and it spilled all over the tent. It's all over my books and papers. This is the last straw. All I want to do is get well or at least feel like 'me' again (whoever 'me' is). There is an ant in my sock...

Admitting Defeat

So, there I was at another major turning point in my life, saying goodbye once again. But wait! Even though I had a ticket in my hand to fly from Central America where I had been camping for three months back to the United States early the next morning, I was not packed and had absolutely no desire to start packing, much less find a ride to the airport!

"What's up with this?" I thought. "Why don't I want to pack?" Was I being divinely led to stay? Lucas assumed I'd take a plane back to my sister's place. What else could a sick, depressed woman do on her own with no money, no job, and no hope of earning an income because of the myriad of effects caused by PMDD?

Lucas told our friends, "I am going to drive her to the airport tomorrow morning."

"Not so quick, buddy," I thought and prayed to find some way to stay in the tropics for another three months.

"You will fly," I distinctly heard God say, "but not on a plane."

"I will fly wherever You want if You'll make a way," I reluctantly agreed. Finally, there was peace in my heart. That night, I slept like a baby.

I had no idea *why* I wanted to camp in Central America for another three months of tropical heat, snakes, mosquitoes, and chiggers, especially after telling my sister I was coming back. But I *knew* the Eternal One was commanding me to stay and fly. Moreover, with that command came His promise to provide what I needed to accomplish His purpose. I decided to try out my butterfly wings.

"Just living isn't enough,"
said the butterfly.
"One must have sunshine,
freedom,
and a little flower."

Hans Christian Anderson

Chapter 5 – Woman on a Mission

"What in the world am I doing?" I asked myself in disbelief as I hurriedly packed an overnight bag. I knew there was a real possibility that I would not be able to make the trip to the border required to renew my tourist visa in one day. I was determined to stay in the tropics for another three months, for a reason that I did not know.

My not-so-rational resolve reminded me of when I once completed a half-marathon without training for it. Just finishing that race gave me the confidence I needed to return to my home and tell my husband that he was right – I did *not* love his computer addiction; I would pack my bags as he had commanded me to and leave peacefully.

Being reminded of such confidence-building incidents made finishing a simple 'marathon' to the border and back, even with a serious language barrier, seem less daunting. The tone of my self-talk thus changed from scolding myself to over-confidence. "I have done plenty of border crossings in other countries. Why not here?" That journey in late January is a happy blur in my memory.

My Father's Angels

While waiting for one of the buses I needed to take to the border, I noticed a slim, older man with a grey ponytail and intense hazel eyes. I could not tell if he was a tourist or a local. He was dressed like a local, and he appeared to speak Spanish fluently. However, when he spoke to me later, he also spoke English perfectly.

"Which bus are you taking?" he asked. I told him where I was going, and we made small talk until our bus arrived. I was happy to let him take the lead and ask the driver all the right questions. We were indeed on the right bus. Having already introduced ourselves, it seemed only appropriate to sit together.

The hours with my 'bi-lingual bus buddy' flew by as our conversation flowed freely from one topic to another – sharing life histories, interests, ideas, travel stories, and family backgrounds.

"Am I talking too much?" Alex kept asking. I was wondering the same thing about myself. I am usually much more reserved with strangers; but for some reason, with Alex, it was different. It felt good to share things with a listening human being after many years of keeping them bottled up.

Later that day, with tourist visas renewed, we found ourselves on a bus headed home. When we were safely back in the country, it was too late to travel back to my campsite, so I asked him, "Do you know any cheap hotels here on the border where I can stay tonight?"

He asked politely, "Would it be inappropriate for me to invite you to stay at my house? It's simple, and it is not very clean, but you're welcome."

Relieved by the offer since it was dark already, I wearily replied, "That would be great."

His La-Z-Boy chair ended up being uncomfortable for me so, at some point during the night, I transferred myself to a little sofa, ungracefully draping my long legs and big feet over the telephone which sat on the end table. The mosquitoes and I slept in that position for the remainder of the night.

***

In the morning, after exchanging pleasantries, Alex said, "Amazing! I didn't hear a single mosquito in my bedroom last night, and I normally do."

I just smiled, thinking to myself, "That's because they were all out here in the living room nibbling on *me*!"

I was ravenously hungry by then, as we had hardly eaten anything the day before. Alex prepared an unforgettable, super-tasty raw breakfast full of fresh bananas and raw cacao from trees in his yard and other delectable tropical treats. Soon I had to catch my bus for the long ride home.

As we parted company, I sensed a deep sadness coming over Alex, and I realized for the first time the significance of my rather abrupt departure. I gave him an impromptu hug (and a little tip) for his kindness in taking all the stress out of my quest for a passport stamp and for making the journey much more enjoyable.

I saw his eyes fill with tears and wondered why. Later, Alex confessed, "You were an answer to prayer."

When I finally arrived home, exhausted from the journey, I flopped down onto my sleeping pad, thankful to see the moon and stars still overhead.

"Thank you, Father, for sending Alex at just the right time," I prayed wearily, "and such a nice angel too."

In No Man's Land

The next day was the first Sabbath I had celebrated *alone* with the Creator in several years. I had tested my butterfly wings for a couple of days and discovered that they were functional, so I happily fluttered around outside my tent. I sat down in the bright sunshine with my face turned upwards in praise to the One who had created the sun. It was such a blessing to be quiet and still and at peace with my Maker and myself. When I later strolled around my campsite, feeling the warm breeze gently caressing me, my spirit soared higher and higher.

I then walked down to the lower camp where the men were having a Bible study together.

"Come and join us," Lucas invited.

I politely declined. "Thanks, but I will go back up to my camp," I said with confidence. That felt so good, just to be able to assert some independence and meet my own need for solitude. I had said 'no' and survived!

***

The next afternoon, an incredible offer was presented to me – one that sounded too good to be true. Tim had a vacant house up in the mountain near a waterfall on his property, and he offered to let me stay there rent free for a short period of time. I would have to live on bananas, but that was a small price to pay for peace and privacy.

In my soggy tent that same evening, I could not sleep so decided to listen to a Scripture song on my laptop.

"Which song?" I indifferently asked the Eternal One.

"Isaiah 60:1," came the distinct answer.

I highlighted the title of the song and hit Enter. I heard, "Arise, *shine*, for thy Light is come, and the glory of the Lord is risen upon thee." It was reassuring to know that I was not alone – the Father of Lights was still with me.

Nearly a week had gone by since I had announced I would stay for another three months, and even though I was still unsettled and lacking the basic comforts of life, I was thoroughly enjoying using my own wings. They would grow stronger with use.

Princess in Paradise

By the time I woke up the next morning, it was almost 6 a.m., too late to catch the bus out of the valley into the city to get supplies. My next alternative for the day was to head up the mountain to see the house that Tim had said was available. Yes, I'd go and check it out for myself. I was feeling upbeat and energetic, optimistic that this was *the* place – my healing sanctuary. I knew before I even saw it.

Upon arrival at the rancho on the mountain, Carlos, the gardener (who spoke Spanish but no English), gave me a quick tour of the organic greenhouse and garden which were below the house and plucked a few leaves from various edible plants for me to enjoy. He knew I was interested in going up to see the house itself, but he motioned for me to pray with him first.

Taking off his gardening hat, Carlos knelt and motioned for me to do the same. He prayed in Spanish, respectfully gazing upward. I sensed the presence of the Most High God during that heartfelt prayer.

We ventured up to see the house which, although in dire need of a deep cleaning, was perfect for my immediate needs – a spacious wooden platform with no walls or doors, an open kitchen with a double stainless steel sink and running water (after Carlos kindly repaired the tap), a spectacular view of the coastline and valley, silence and solitude, birds and butterflies, a garden to tend, an outhouse, and all the bananas I could eat. My heavenly Father had provided the perfect place.

I nearly ran down the mountain to share the good news with Tim, the owner, the one who had offered me this bountiful blessing in my hour of need.

Several hours later, in the heat of the day, I had my old campsite all tidied up and headed up the mountain with as much as I could carry – my tent, a foam mattress, a small bag of overnight necessities slung over my shoulder, and blankets for the cool tropical nights. Stopping every 10 stairs or so to catch my breath, I was soon soaked with perspiration in the heat, but I was happy, oh, so happy! What a miracle – from 'lost and homeless' to 'grounded with a palace' in less than 24 hours! How blessed I was.

Yes, I felt like a princess in a filthy palace, but I was so grateful to have a place of my own to clean. While sweeping, mopping, and de-cobwebbing, I was singing for the first time in years with only the local howler monkeys to hear my voice!

As I worked around the wooden platform, I removed some decorative items left by a previous resident, carefully placing them inside a bag for their owner. As I took the final item from the shelf and placed it in the bag, I saw something standing directly behind it — a small oval piece of wood, colorfully hand painted with the word, 'SHINE.'

I remembered the song the Eternal had given me just a few nights before, Isaiah 60:1, "Arise, *shine*, for thy light is come…"

SHINE. Here it was again. Surely, the Creator was with me in that healing haven — a tranquil garden sanctuary.

***

Suddenly I thought back to when I had first arrived in Central America and was staying with the family at the seaport. One day their 7-year-old daughter wrote a letter to me in Spanish, "You are a *shining* light in our home."

"A *shining* light?" I had thought to myself at the time. This was not *my* doing. Only the heavenly Light can empower a woman who has suffered depression for most of her adult life to be a light for others.

When I went back to my tent that day, I fell to my knees, gratefully and humbly acknowledging my Source of strength.

Just a few days after reading that little girl's letter, while I was still living with her family, I was strolling along the beach so Weepy Wanda could visit privately. I was inspecting the flotsam and jetsam that the tide was bringing in. It was the usual driftwood, coconuts, small shells, a bloated fish, a blue plastic shoe, and so on. Then I noticed there were several glass bottles on the shore within a few feet of each other.

"Wouldn't it be funny," I thought to myself, "if God would send me a message in a bottle?" I almost laughed aloud at the thought. Then half seriously, I stopped and prayed silently, "Eternal God, would you send me a message in a bottle, something to remind me that You are with me even when I am depressed, when I feel that ending my life is a better option than existing in the endless darkness?"

Immediately, I was filled with remorse for praying like this. Chiding myself for presenting such a silly request before the sacred throne of the Eternal, I began having negative thoughts like, "Why would He do something so special for someone like me?" and "It was so presumptuous and arrogant for me to make a request like that!"

I timidly glanced around at the big glass bottles on the beach, hoping to see something inside one of them but not really expecting to. Seconds later, I noticed a small plastic shampoo bottle inches away from where I was standing. Something (or Someone) prompted me to bend down and turn the bottle over.

"But I can see there is nothing inside it," I protested silently. "There is no message in that bottle." Even so, without a bit of faith, I obeyed, feeling completely foolish as I did so. I picked up the old shampoo bottle and turned it over to see the label on the other side. The name of the shampoo was 'SHINE.' There was my 'message in a bottle!'

With tears of gratitude, I fell on my knees, thanking the Eternal God for His faithfulness to me. He had heard my prayer and answered my childlike request.

Getting up from where I had been kneeling in the sand, I continued my conversation with the Creator. Even after that encounter, my faith was still weak.

"Would it be presumptuous, Father," I prayed, "to ask for another favor?" I knew in the bottom of my heart that He had already given me, in the message on the shampoo bottle, so much more than I deserved. Even so, I very hesitantly presented my request. "I know that with You all things are possible, so would you plant a heart-shaped rock here on the beach that I can give to Lucas to remind him of Your love for him?"

Again, I half-heartedly kept an eye open for a special rock for the next couple of minutes, again not believing that I would actually find one. And I did not. However, I was not disappointed because I had prayed without faith yet again. It served me right for the Almighty to ignore my request. I gave up looking for the rock.

I continued my walk along the beach until I found a path leading inland which would take me to the road for the homeward journey. As I left the beach, my eyes were drawn to an ordinary piece of driftwood in the sand. When I set my umbrella on the wood so I could take out my camera, I noticed a rock that had been intentionally placed on that driftwood. What shape was the rock? Yes, of course, *heart-shaped* – the rock I had asked for.

I had expected the Father to answer my prayer for the heart-shaped rock in the same way He had answered the one for the message in a bottle – immediately. Instead, in His own time, when it was unexpected, He joyfully planted a rock that could not be missed.

Prayer for Peace

The next morning, after my first solid night's rest in the open-air rancho, I woke up with no headache for a change. I was in a good mood and raring to go. However, I was hungry so I decided to head back down to civilization for some groceries. (There is no Safeway in the jungle.)

Before I reached the highway, two little friends greeted me in my new garden paradise, so I did not feel lonely. The first was a green inchworm which had found its way onto my clothes and seemed to wave to me a cheery hello. The second was a coati (of the raccoon family). A big, furry thing, the coati was running around sniffing everywhere, his tail up in the air like a flag. He did not appear to fear me at all, only curious.

When I got down to Tim's place, he was arranging for a friend to take his car into town for tire realignment, so Tim asked me if I wanted to ride along.
"Sure," I said, "a ride would be great."

Tim's friend and I went up to the house to get the vehicle that needed realignment. There I met another angel, a young woman from Texas named Lauren. She and her new husband of three days – a sweet young Christian couple – were on their honeymoon and planning to hike up to 'my' waterfall with Tim's son that day.

After we talked a bit, I felt comfortable enough to share about my depression.

After sharing some of her own story, Lauren asked, "May I pray for you?

Lauren stood beside me and, placing her hand gently on my shoulder, prayed one of the most beautiful prayers I have heard, claiming promises from Scripture for my direction and healing and peace. She moved her hand onto my bowed head and continued. I felt so loved, so special – a sick and tired old woman feeling as young and beautiful as a princess. That was a special blessing for that day and for my life.

On the way into town, I had an opportunity to talk to Tim's ex-wife without Tim or Lucas around and shared a few details about PMDD with her. I also mentioned cleaning the rancho and my willingness to make grass juice for the tourists passing by the garden on their way to the waterfall. Then I volunteered to help Carlos in the organic garden sometimes.

When I finished, she asked what was becoming a recurring question, "How long will you stay up there?"
"As long as it's good for everyone," I answered, which was the truth. There was no lease or rental agreement, just a simple understanding that I needed a place to heal that was away from stress and people (especially emotional

vampires), having just struck out on my own with no income or financial support.

Tim's friend dropped me off on a corner somewhere downtown. Along the way, I decided I needed more than a couple hours in town because I did not know my way around and had quite a list of things to buy to get myself established up on the mountain. "I will come back by myself on the bus," I told him.

I had no idea where I was, but using a big church as a landmark, I started wandering around the city. Thankfully, I was just a few steps away from a large market where I knew I could find a traditional hot cooked breakfast – gallo pinto (rice and beans). Good-natured, the waitress was patient with me when I told her that I did not speak Spanish and had to order in English, and in a short time I was guzzling down a glass of orange juice followed by a large plate of food.

With renewed energy and enthusiasm, I hit the streets again. Soon, I was ready to catch the bus for the return journey to the village and then up into the jungle to my camp. I was carrying bags full of dry goods, including several notebooks for my writing, reminiscent of the 'good old days' before computers when everything was handwritten. I had also bought a new eraser, just as if I were going back to school.

I knew if the bus did not reach the top of the hill by 4 p.m., I would not have time to make it into the valley (about an hour's walk) and up to the rancho (another hour's hike up the mountain) before dark. I prayed for a car to give me a lift between the top of the hill and Tim's house. This would buy me some daylight.

Two vehicles passed me, but both were full. A motorbike whizzed by, but the driver did not stop, and since it was not an emergency, I did not flag him down. I fully expected to sleep at the basecamp overnight and then head up the mountain the next morning. That's when my second angel of the day appeared. A 4x4 pulled up onto the gravel road. The driver looked undecided for a moment, and then he turned my direction. I knew he would stop for me.

"Where are you headed?" he asked. It was a foreigner who spoke English! He told me he was head to the community right beside Tim's house.

"That's perfect," I said in disbelief. "Could I get a lift?"

"Of course. Jump in."

His young son, who was sitting in a car seat in the back, asked me, "Would you like some plantain chips?" He was such a polite little boy, almost angelic. I learned that his name was Gabriel. (Yes, *really!*)

"No, but thanks for offering," I answered Gabriel, still amazed at his good manners. And thanks to my 'angels', I had plenty of time to get home before dark.

One of the highlights of that trip to town was spending an hour at the internet café and reading a long email from Alex down on the border. He had written how much he had enjoyed being together and of his plans to come visit me. It was then that I realized that Alex was seeing me in a very different light than I was seeing him.

Remembering that I had slept in his living room, my reply to him had very clear statements about not looking for a boyfriend carefully woven into the message.

"…Saying to those who are bound, "Come out!';
to those who are in darkness, 'Show yourselves!'

Isaiah 49:9a

Chapter 6 – It's My Party

That was my first full day alone in my new healing haven. I cleaned all day until about mid-afternoon when I broke away from the dust long enough to hike up to the caves. Then I climbed down to the swimming hole for a cold, refreshing dip, breathing the wonderfully powerful negative ions from the waterfall, and enjoying the frigid of water pounding on my head.

The next day was stressful because it was spent on the internet at Tim's place where I was trying to concentrate amidst all the commotion in and around the house. There was another email from Alex.

I felt sorry for him, the poor, lonely man. He needed friends. I thought that his spending a week or so at Tim's place might benefit him. Since he could speak Spanish, he could also talk to Time and Carlos. So, I replied to Alex's email with my own invitation to come visit us.

Thoughts on the Loose

My heart was beginning to soften toward Alex. I really did not know what to do with him since I hardly knew him:

2/3/12 – Eternal God, I am so thankful to wake up in the middle of the night (never mind that I must march myself to the outhouse) and have this quiet place all to myself. I am disturbing no one; and more importantly, no one is disturbing me. I can crunch through the dry leaves without a second thought about whom I might wake besides any snakes or nocturnal creatures I may meet along the way. I can sit in the loft and gaze at the stars without needing to consider whom I will rouse when I lay back down in the tent.

Alex misses his twice-a-day communication with his former girlfriend of four years now that she is in the big city. However, I don't understand why she did not explain to him why she was leaving. Where will he stay if he comes to visit? Will his smoking be an issue? Do I want him to visit my peaceful place knowing what I know about his intention to find a woman? What can I say or do to discourage him from pursuing a love relationship without hurting him and convince him that he needs a whole community of support rather than just one person? Why do I have such a healing burden for a man I spent a mere 24 hours with? Indeed, what can I do to help him?

Lucas has only three or four more weeks on his visa. Will he go to the border and re-enter for another three months like I did?

Later – *Tried to go back to sleep, but it's impossible. Still thinking about Alex. I must stay focused. My only duty right now is to heal myself. I know it's natural for women to feel honored and flattered when men take special notice of us and tell us that they like what they see. Yes, it feels good. But for me, it feels even better to have a man ask about me – not only my past and where I have been, but to express an interest in who I am now and what my dreams are by asking open-ended questions. Our conversation was so natural and spontaneous when we were traveling together. I enjoy his presence – a gentle, secure, non-threatening, encouraging, peaceful presence for a change.*

2/4/12 – Woke up in tears after a very real nightmare. But the tears lasted only for a moment when I looked outside the tent and recognized my surroundings. Afterall, I was waking up in a modern-day Garden of Eden! Birds were chattering away in the trees, and the early morning horizon was bright with hope of a better day.

I am happy to be here, happy to be alive, happy to be free, happy that I did not take my life in December (or any of those awful days, weeks, and months that I wanted to kill myself). The Eternal has kept me alive for this moment, to have the delight of watching me treasure this tropical paradise, delighting myself in His creative presence.

The nightmare I had was all too real. My husband was driving me to the airport. He told me he did not want me around anymore, so I had to go somewhere. In the dream, I was going to miss my flight to freedom, and my husband was dilly dallying, searching for his glasses, driving painfully slow while I, on the other hand, felt like I was having a heart attack, knowing I had bags to check and only minutes to spare before the flight left. Then we almost got stopped by a policeman because my husband could not find his seat belt. I learned that we had to cross an international border to get to the airport, and then I *knew* we would not make it in time for me to catch my flight as neither of us had a passport!

"I am going to take a taxi," I announced, since the police would be less likely to stop a speeding taxi on the highway. But my husband refused to stop and let me out. I thought about bailing out at a stoplight, but then I'd have to leave my bags behind. Suddenly a sickening thought crossed my mind. I realized my husband was purposely keeping me in the car against my will. He was holding me hostage.

"You booked the airline ticket, so it's *your* fault our marriage broke up," he said, continuing to pour on the guilt.

When I realized it was over (both our marriage and any hope of getting away from him), I started to cry.

Apparently, the crying upset him because he stopped the car and shoved me out the door. He roared off in a cloud of dust. I lay hurt and helpless on the side of the highway, with nothing and no one.

In the dream, I found myself on the steps of a church. Eventually, a priest drove up and walked up the steps to where I was lying, in obvious pain. He was holding a stack of tithe receipts which he was waiting for his parishioners to come and take from him one by one. The priest indicated that he would help after he had passed out all his papers, but other than that, he just ignored me. The people receiving their tithe receipts also ignored my plight.

In the dream, I was still lying on the ground sobbing my eyes out, but it was as if I were invisible. Without hope or comfort, feeling half-dead already, I just wanted to die for good. That is when I woke up crying.

Then this promise came to my mind, *"Yahweh, your God, is among you, a mighty one who will save. He will rejoice over you with joy. He will calm you in his love. He will rejoice over you with singing." (Zephaniah 3:17).*

Later that day, I wrote in my journal:

Happiness is ...
having free access to greens, especially fresh cilantro
eating a whole avocado in one day
enjoying a fresh papaya for breakfast
making a bowl of oats and plantain with flax
watching a shining blue butterfly in the garden
feeling a freshly mopped wooden floor, cool under my feet
listening to the howler monkeys in the distance
watching a pineapple grow bigger day after day
having teeth to chew raw carrots
eating flavorful tomatoes
having fresh flowers with which to decorate the rancho
knowing there is an icy shower after I hike up here
thinking about a visit from Alex, my travel buddy

Later that night, as the sun was setting, I wrote:

Stillness, misty silence
Solitude, cricket choir
Gentle rain nearby
Darkness falls
Earth rests
Lights from the valley
Like fireflies through the fog
Stillness
A leaf falls
Breaking the misty silence
Birds are in bed
A heavy truck on the highway below
A dog barking far in the distance
Another leaf falls
Listening for the Eternal's voice
Evening coolness
Time for socks and light

A candle
It's Sabbath
Drip, drop, slow rain
I am dry and thankful
Flickering flame
Warm and bright
Cheering glow
Shining Light!

Meeting Mr. Carl the Coati Again

At this point in my blissful solitude, any diversion was appreciated, even if it was in the form of a furry visitor:

2/4/12 – An early start to the day.... I heard noises and felt something thud somewhere downstairs – the whole lower floor vibrated. Assuming it was not a person (who would hike up my mountain in the dark?), I went downstairs with my flashlight to investigate. I saw that the bananas I had hung from the roof the day before were gone. I directed the beam of my headlamp a few feet from the house, and there was Mr. Coati feasting on my bananas. What nerve! I clapped my hands to scare him off, but he continued munching. I clapped again. No response. So, I left him where he was and gave up on having that bunch of bananas for breakfast.

Bananas on the Brain

2/5/12 – Mr. Coati came to visit again last night. I was around dusk this time, a bit earlier than the previous visit. I was glad to see a familiar face, but I would not mind if it were not so furry. He knew exactly where to look for bananas, but I was smart and had hidden them in a 5-gallon

*pail with a lid so he did not find any. I learned my lesson —
do not leave bananas out overnight if you want any for
breakfast in the morning!*

*2/6/12 — Mr. Coati was back again this morning. It did not
matter how much I shouted, clapped, or stomped, he was
determined to get the bananas I was going to eat for
breakfast. Maybe I should just feed him. It's obvious he is
not going away anytime soon. And with no doors, walls, or
windows, I cannot very well shut him out.*

*I will call him Carl the coati for now. I don't think Carl is a
stranger here. He climbed up onto the kitchen sink easily
and wandered all overlooking for the bananas that I had
closed up with my other food. Then I swallowed my
breakfast before he had a chance to grab my plate of raw
oats and bananas. I think he'll be back.*

*9:00 a.m. — Sure enough, Carl came back. He smelled the
banana peels in my compost bucket and rolled it about 15
feet away from the house, trying to pry off the lid, but he
was unsuccessful.*

*12:00 Noon — Carl was back, but he did not stay long when
he saw that raw cabbage and raw green beans were on the
menu. I think he is growing on me.*

*It's raining again and very misty, even in the rancho. I feel
like I am sitting inside a cloud. I am all wrapped up in a
blanket, daydreaming. I am thankful to know I am beloved
of God and can rest in His arms rather than fall into yet
another relationship.*

Men Again

One of the biggest challenges of living at the rancho in the jungle was being totally off the grid yet needing internet to keep in touch with family and friends back home and to do research for my book manuscript. I met the challenge by using Tim's Wi-Fi once a week and then made small donations toward this service. Coming down from my castle in the clouds to use the internet brought me out of my mountain retreat occasionally.

By this time, I was already tapering off my Prozac:

2/6/12 – Went down to civilization today and used the internet for nearly five hours with barely a break. That was exhausting. Mostly happy stuff like chatting with my sister on Skype, doing research for the book manuscript, and emailing Alex to work out the details of his visit.

As I was hiking back up to the gardens, I bumped into a young Israeli man sitting along the trail. He looked like he was ready to give up hiking to the waterfall. I encouraged him to keep going and traded my walking sticking for his guitar as we continued up the trail together. We joined up with another young man along the way who was hiking barefoot. The three of us went on our merry way and soon caught up with three more adults and two children. When we reached the gardens, we all hung out together for a while, and I shared some bananas with the hikers. That was fun.

There was a long email waiting for me from Alex. He is serious about coming here but did not give a reason for coming or a length of time that he would stay. I am looking forward to seeing him again and sharing some time together. I pray my mood cooperates and that I do not tumble down into the valley of darkness when he is here. The timing is right that I could be heading downhill emotionally from next week onwards, but maybe there is still enough Prozac in me to keep me level, at least while Alex is around.

11:30 p.m. – I feel a bit lower tonight – tomorrow is a Prozac morning. My drug days are almost over... I am terrified of falling into that big black hole again.

"The people who walked in darkness
have seen a great light.
The light has shined on those who lived
in the land of the shadow of death."

Isaiah 9:2

Chapter 7 – Renewed Hope

My energy had remained quite high for some time, and I was optimistic that things were changing for the better as far as my mental health was concerned:

2/8/12 – It's hard to believe that I can visualize a future for myself. It has been such a long time since I have dared to dream or had the energy to think forward like this. It's a scary place, so alien and unfamiliar to me. Oh, Yahweh, You alone can make it happen! You created me and know what it takes to restore me – a miracle.

Speaking of miracles, I am watching a pineapple grow before my very eyes, right in front of the platform where I sit to write in the morning. Amazing fruit! Amazing Creator!

I took a shower up near the rancho today. The water is piped down from a mountain stream – felt a bit glacial, but it was invigorating! My shower was not exactly private either (unless one considers hiding behind banana plants as being private) but it's running water and for that I am grateful.

Shining for God's Glory

My thoughts turned toward Alex more and more as we continued our infrequent emails arranging for his visit:

2/9/12, Midnight – I woke up thinking about Alex again. I wish I were healed and whole and had something to offer the man. I am too sick to be in a special relationship with anyone right now. He is such a nice man. For some reason, I feel very comfortable in his presence. Maybe that's it: he is older and wiser, like an uncle or a favorite teacher. He is like a comfortable pair of well-worn slippers – warm, fuzzy, and safe. However, that is not exactly the way he seems to be viewing me. Is there any way to meet in the middle? I guess I will find out when he gets here.

The star-studded sky fills me with wonder. There are thousands, no tens of thousands, of sparkling, twinkling stars.

El Olam [Eternal God], what do you mean when You keep telling me to shine? Do You want me to shine like a full moon on a clear night? Or the sun at noonday in the heat? Or like the sun in its brilliance after a thunderstorm? And surely, I am not just shining for myself? The sun blesses others with its warmth and light. Who do You want me to bless when I shine?

***

While I was down at Tim's to use the internet this afternoon, I told Lucas about Alex's visit next week.

"Did you send him a 'Dear John' letter already?" was his only response.

"Yes," I answered truthfully.

"On second thought, that may not be enough," Lucas shook his head.

"What's it to Lucas?" I thought to myself. "Whether this guy likes me or not is none of his business."
In his email today, Alex confirmed his visit and where we will meet, etc. I am so excited! When we parted two weeks ago

(has it only been two weeks since I said goodbye to a gloomy man at the bus terminal?), I never expected to see him again. Lucas is thinking about driving to the city just to meet Alex at the bus terminal. What a nosy body he is!

I am enjoying every last second of the fading sun. I am thrilled, joyed to my core, that I can sit here in the stillness with my Creator watching this glorious sunset that He painted for me tonight. The colors are always such a miraculous display, especially here in the tropics.

I Prayed for Death but was Given New Life

When I returned to the rancho, some Scripture promises flooded my mind, one after another, in response to the negative thoughts from the past:

I said, "I am confused!"
His Word to me: "I am the way, the truth, and the life" (John 14:6a).

I said, "I hate myself!"
His Word to me: "I have loved you with an everlasting love" (Jeremiah 31:3a).

I said, "I am angry!"
His Word to me: "My peace I give unto you" (John 14:27).

I said, "I can't get up!"
His Word to me: "Arise, shine; for your light has come, and Yahweh's glory has risen on you" (Isaiah 60:1).

I said, "It's impossible!"

His Word to me: "With God all things are possible"
(Matthew 19:26).

I said, "It's so dark!"
His Word to me: "I am the light of the world" (John 8:12).

I said, "It's hopeless!"
His Word to me: "May the God of hope fill you with all joy
and peace..." (Romans 15:13).

I said, "I want to die!"
His Word to me: "I am the resurrection and the life" (John
11:25).

"Death," I pleaded. "Diamonds," God smiled.

2/11/12 – My thoughts are coming so fast and furious that
my stubby little pencil cannot keep up. It's 9 a.m. and I am
savoring the sights and sounds. Feel deeply, my soul! The
rushing waterfall, the birds, cicadas, mosquitoes in my ear,
and all the lush foliage surroundings against a clear blue sky
– all of these are God's diamonds for me.

2/12/12, Morning – Getting more and more excited about
seeing Alex tomorrow. I pray it goes as planned.

Dawn and Disappointment

I had decided that Alex's visit was a good thing after all and
was now overexcited about his arrival:

2/13/12 – Today's the day, finally. The waiting is almost
over. Now I am counting hours instead of days....

4:30 a.m. – In the past, when Weepy Wanda and Fatigued Francine were often around, I probably would have avoided going to the city because of the noise and commotion. Eternal God, I praise You for these good days in Your light and that I feel like making the trek into the city to meet Alex.

1:30 p.m. – So much for Valentine's Day tomorrow. I went to the bus station and waited for Alex; but when person after person disembarked, and Alex and his signature ponytail did not appear, my heart sank. I guess I set myself up for a hard fall. I do not even have the motivation to go back to the café and email my disappointment to Alex and my frustration to Lucas. So what if I spent a day cleaning and raking around the rancho for his arrival, pitching my tent outside so he could use the platform, and taking a long journey through the dark jungle amidst a pack of howler monkeys to catch the bus to the city? I sure don't want to make the trip into the city again for a long time! I don't understand why Alex did not email me about not coming as planned. If Weepy Wanda were with me today, I'd be crying right now. So, my focus goes off Alex's visit – he'll come when he is ready, when the time is right. Now I can focus on my book again.

6:30 p.m. – I am so grateful to have this beautiful, tranquil place to come home to. Makes life worth living, meeting the Eternal here every night and every morning with songs of praise. When I think where I could be and remember where I have been and what I was looking forward to just a few short weeks ago, wow, what a miracle has taken place! Yahweh, I told You it would take a miracle and You gave me one!

Valentine's Day

I did not know why Alex had not shown up as planned, but I was upset that I had made the long trip into the city unnecessarily, draining both my finances and my time. I wanted to know what had happened:

2/14/12, 2:15 a.m. – I love to wake up out here in my tent and see the shadow of the leaves from the sweet lemon tree on the tent walls, from the bright moon shining through them – a kind of leafy wallpaper.

Eternal One, I know that the mystery of the missing man (Alex) is part of Your plan, for whatever reason. May he be blessed.

6 a.m. – Couldn't go back to sleep. I can tell it's going to be another doozy of a day. I hope either Alex or Lucas communicated with me last night by email and apologizes for the mix up. I'd feel a whole lot better!

7:15 p.m. – Tried to call Alex twice today, morning and late afternoon. I finally reached him a few hours ago and found out where the miscommunication occurred. He told me that Lucas had called him early Sunday morning and told him not to come as planned because Lucas was going to the city for a while. Alex assumed that Lucas would convey the change of plans to me, but he did not. I could tell Alex felt bad about the miscommunication. I have heard nothing from the guilty party – sweet, thoughtful Lucas. Raging Rhonda is someone nearby.

"He reveals the deep and secret things. He knows what is in the darkness, and the light dwells with him."

Daniel 2:22

Chapter 8 – Castle in the Clouds

At the beginning of my time living at the rancho, I never intended to write a book about my experience with PMDD. However, by this point, I was already motivated, scribbling into a notebook that rested on one of the treads of the spiral staircase up to the loft. That tread was my 'desk,' and I sat on a broken plastic chair beneath it. Ergonomic? Definitely not, but page after page flowed from that stubby pencil.

About a week into writing the manuscript, something happened that greatly increased my motivation:

2/16/12 – This is incredible! A big group came up this morning and wandered around in the garden for a while. Then their guide brought them up to the house. I was upstairs writing but went downstairs to be sociable. The conversation got around to what I do here, and I decided to bring up my book. It just gushed out of me, and I was able to direct the conversation to the Creator, the Eternal, who has blessed me so abundantly. It felt so natural to go from "it's about female depression" to more specific information such as "PMDD affects about 3-8% of females." I need to decide on the title fast!

It was a joyous uplift to have something positive to share with the women in the group, but all of them, male and female, were listening intently. They started talking about people they know who are depressed. Praise God for such a positive first experience!

6:30 p.m. – Just returned from an expedition down to Tim's to get my avocados and tomatoes for this week. Enjoyed the trek back up here, although I ate only one banana before hitting the trail. My stamina lasted longer today, my steps were more confident than when I first moved up here. Am I developing mountain legs?

***

While I was down there, Lucas asked me, "Where is the $200 I gave you?"

"That is long gone," I said.

"What are you using to live on?" he wanted to know.

"I have a bit in my bank account from selling some of my stuff on eBay."

He said, "Maybe I can hire you to do some typing."

"Maybe, but I am busy with my book right now."

Does he expect me to say I need his money? No way! He had plenty of opportunity to help me before – it's too late now. I'd rather beg on the streets than take his money.

Butterflies

2/18/12 – At the entrance of the front garden today, an orange butterfly met me as if to say, "I'm glad you're here!" I feel so at home and calm on the mountain, unlike 'down there' where everything is muddled up for me. Minimalism is healing – simple, natural, tranquil, silent, unhurried, serene, nonaggressive, nonconfrontational, noncombative.

I am feeling tired and low energy and a bit nauseous this morning. Maybe it's from the walk or lack of sleep. Or maybe the busy week is catching up with me and being around people so much. Or maybe the late, cooked dinner that tasted so good last night is attacking my digestive system. Or maybe my aching back is telling me I have some sort of flu.

When I went to the cave this morning, I noticed the rainbow at the bottom of the falls. (I couldn't even hear the locusts over the thunderous water.) Then I saw a blue butterfly in front of the waterfall — a shining one — just for me. It was brilliant, almost blinding, as it floated against the backdrop of the dark green jungle foliage. And the Creator wants me to shine like one of these?!

More notes from the waterfall expedition:

11:30 a.m. — I brought Alex to the waterfall with me in my mind today. He is such a private person — I think he would really enjoy it up here. I pray that the Eternal will give him the motivation and power to quit smoking once and for all. What if lung cancer takes away the only friend I have right now?

Later — *Thinking about Alex again. Maybe he'll just be an acquaintance in my life — you know, one of those angels who is in and out, making a big impact when they are around but quickly gone — especially if I only stay in this country until the end of the summer and never return. Wouldn't it be funny if both of us are butterflies?*

Like most people, I think, I long to have a companion to share life with, but so far, I keep attaching myself to 'unsafe' people who do not respect my boundaries and who are more interested in what I can do for them than in who I am as a person. That is so sad. I want to be me and feel safe being me.

Eternal God, let Alex be an example of a safe man in my life. That is a high expectation of a person, but I believe he can live up to it without even knowing that I want this. I need relationships with emotionally healthy people.

I must be tired today because I am thinking of all the reasons I will not be able to finish my book and then get it edited and published. Am I being realistic and rational when I have these thoughts, or is it Wanda and her friends creeping up on me?

Counting the Hours

A week had passed, and Alex had rescheduled his visit for the next day. I was not quite as excited as the previous week, but still happier than a monkey in a fruit tree:

2/18/12 – The birds are chirping. My headache appears to be gone. Nine hours of sleep. Not sure I feel like raking today, especially heavy, wet leaves. Another trip to the outhouse.... Maybe I will go look for monkeys while I am down near the shed.

Hard to believe a week has already flown by and Alex is due to arrive tomorrow. I am tempted to take the bus into the city again to meet him and have a few extra hours together, but I really don't need anything from town, so it would be a waste of money that I do not have. Besides, I am still exhausted from the last trip!

The Angel's Arrival

2/20/12 Night – Finally! Alex is here! It's hard to believe it has only been three weeks since we traveled together. When Alex got off the bus, I helped him with his bags and then gave him a hug. Lucas and Tim came to meet Alex when he was putting up his tent, which I thought was nice of them. I will sleep at the basecamp tonight. Alex will be fine with the guys – they went to town tonight to find an ATM and some groceries. I pray something good comes out of this trip for Alex.

The major highlight of the day (besides Alex's arrival) – I started typing the book manuscript when I was plugged in!

He's a Giver, He's a Gift

2/21/12 – Can't sleep. It's after midnight and I have been up for an hour. Lovely calm evening, hardly a breeze. Stars twinkling in the dark night sky, and here I am, still trying to figure out how to get this book typed with no access to electricity without seeing Lucas and the whirlwind of activity and commotion at the base of the mountain. I am itching to have power up here at the rancho without buying a $600 solar power pack. At the rate I am going, there is no way I can have the manuscript typed by June as I had hoped; that would be unrealistic. And I definitely do not want money from Lucas.

All I want is to sleep in my own bed, work in the garden, and write this book. This may be a good healing environment, but unless I can get internet and computer access figured out soon, it will not be a place I can publish my book from.

"Eternal God, help me know what I can do to make progress with this, Your project. You told me to shine. I want to share my story and bring hope to other women, but how without a computer? Please show me the way."

"I will turn their mourning into joy,
and will comfort them,
and make them rejoice
from their sorrow."

Jeremiah 31:13

Chapter 9 – Facing My Fears

The days were passing gently by, and I was overjoyed with my new daily routine and sunny living situation. It was such a blessing to feel positive emotions again after all that I had been through:

2/23/12, 3:30 a.m. – It's windy and clear outside this morning, thousands of tiny stars dotting the clear night sky. The tarp on the rancho is billowing in the wind like a sail on a ship, and so are the sides of my tent. Every gust reminds me I am sleeping outside in the Creator's beautiful nature.

When I told Lucas that it was over, I meant it. Look at me thrive now! Maybe it's the green jungle environment? Or the raw green diet? Or being true to my heart? Or having a purpose that is larger than I am? Or getting regular and adequate sleep? Or the increased aerobic exercise and sunlight? I don't know, but I sure feel like a different person. Is this what being me feels like? I like me!

I am so thankful to know what joy and happiness feel like again. I can feel pleasure and sadness, see colors, hear sounds, taste flavors, look forward to something, serve people. What a night and day difference! "…Though I was blind, now I see" (John 9:25). The gray flowers are now splashes of vivid colors! The dark, shadowy sun is now intense light! The grey trees are now vibrant shades of green! The silent birds now sing and chirp and warble and coo and twitter and tweet! Beautiful, blessed experience!

No Rest for the Weary

2/24/12 – It's that time of evening when everything begins to glow – the sky turns to gold, the air is cool, the birds say good night to each other, the locusts sing a final twilight chorus, and the sun's rays become soft and intimate. The different shades of green in the foliage are more intense, the butterflies seem to fly a bit slower as they flutter from plant to plant.

I still think about having a special someone who sincerely desires to know me yet one who can truly love me nonetheless. None of the "when you agree with me" stuff or the "when you do what I want you to" stuff or the "when you're happy and pleasant" stuff, but a man who loves me, not a vision of what he thinks I am but for who I really am.

Thank you, Eternal God, for loving me wholly, perfectly, relentlessly, unchangeably, for all eternity.

Later – Almost 10 p.m. and still cannot sleep. I am lying on a couple of foam mats on the upper deck. Alex is outside in the tent on a similar 'bed.' I have been reflecting on the conversation we had tonight after supper, sitting on the deck watching the sunset.

He said several times that he is comfortable talking to me and has never 'talked like this' with any woman, even his girlfriend or his ex-wife. (Or maybe they are just poor listeners?) It was fun for me, mostly light conversation and sharing about ourselves. Alex is rapidly becoming my psychotherapist! Maybe I can hang out at his place part of each month, and we can work on my book together.

Talking with Alex tonight, I realize that I have been depression-free (and without Prozac) for three weeks. But if I leave my healing haven and head back to 'stressville' with people (especially a particular emotional vampire) and commotion and noise and no routine, will I lose what I have gained here?

Candle in the Dark

2/25/12, 11 p.m. – Alex is very much on my mind. We spent a restful day together, but of course I did not get to work on the book. I ran some ideas past Alex which was enormously helpful to me. He may be my best critic because he has never seen me sick.

Remembering Falling Stars

2/26/12, 2 a.m. – I am writing with a pencil that has a broken point again. The lead keeps falling out. Sure looking forward to getting what I have already written typed onto the computer. I have lots of pages to enter!

This morning Alex (with a twinkle in his eye) suggested, "Maybe our friendship is just part of your healing." I cannot say I disagree. Everything he says and does feels so sincere, natural, and safe. He has become my safety net, the string on my kite to keep me grounded as I test out my new wings.

Later – A group of hikers came up the mountain. One man about my age shook my hand and asked, "How long have you been up here?"

"Almost a month," I smiled.

He looked intently at me for a moment and then said with awe in his voice, "I can tell. You're shining!"

*****

Amazingly, Alex and I saw a falling star at the same time when we were together last night. While watching that entire expanse of tropical sky speckled with millions of stars, we both happened to be watching the same section of sky when the star fell.

When Alex told the guys down at Tim's about the falling stars, Lucas broke into song, "When the moon hits your eye like a big pizza pie, that's amoré!" Alex blushed when he told me that.

Healing

2/27/12 – I can scarcely believe what Alex told me yesterday. He said that the other day when he was chatting with Carlos alone in the garden (in Spanish), Carlos said, "You should marry her!" That was a shocker! Carlos probably just thinks I should not be up here on the mountain alone because it is completely isolated if I ever need help in an emergency.

Whenever I think of Alex or I remember Saturday night talking under the stars on the deck, I feel that telltale flutter of my heart. My heart skips beats, and I find myself smiling. What am I going to do with him?

Alex is gentle, practical, a real Teddy bear, comfortable to be around, and encouraging, so meek and mild. Yes, I can honestly say our relationship is a healing one, at least for me. He knows about my 'split personalities' (AKA Wanda, Hannah, Iris, Francine, and Rhonda) and not only has he not run away, but he has, in fact, run toward me.

11:30 a.m. – It has been 24 hours since Alex went down to Tim's place, and I have been counting the hours until I see him again. What's with me? At least talking to him is something to look forward to. Sometimes I do get lonely, although I still prefer silence and solitude.

I am so happy now that sometimes I feel I could burst. Every day when I wake up with no headache, enough energy to get out of bed, and gratitude for the hours of the day ahead that I know will contain some treasure, something beautiful for my pleasure from heaven, I am so thankful to be out of the dungeon!

I realize that I may fall back in the deep, dark hole at any moment, with or without prior warning, but until that happens, I am enjoying being alive, and I am thankful that I did not end it all when I wanted to. Like I wrote before, this garden and waterfall and the Eternal Presence here were worth living for.

It is also worth living to see the joy in Alex's eyes when he is enjoying my companionship. May my life be worthwhile because I have brought a smile to a lonely man's face.

Heading to the Border

It was time for Lucas to renew his visa, and he decided to drive down to the border town where Alex lived. I invited myself along for the ride! I was excited at the thought of spending some time with Alex and having a place with electricity to type my long manuscript pages. And getting a free ride there (albeit with Lucas) instead of contending with the local buses was the cherry on top.

"But those who wait for Yahweh
will renew their strength.
They will mount up with wings like eagles.
They will run, and not be weary.
They will walk, and not faint."

Isaiah 40:31

Chapter 10 – Looking Ahead

The drive to the border with Lucas and Alex must have been an uneventful one because there was no mention of it in my journal. However, I did record a conversation I had with Lucas after we arrived at Alex's house that evening:

2/29/12, 3 a.m. – Sleeping in my tent in Alex's yard and got woken up by the neighbor's rooster again, the one that cannot tell time. I am still counting the hours until I can be alone. I know I should be able to have peace in all situations – that a quiet mind should not be determined by circumstances and people I am with – but it does make a difference.

Lucas was pushing into me again last night. When he offered to rent a cabin for me if I stayed in Central America longer, I declined.

"Why not? You'd have electricity, a washing machine, a hot shower …"

"No, thanks. I just want to be alone. You'd be there."

He pointed at Alex who was on the phone and retorted sarcastically, "Isn't he a person?"

There's a big, big difference between 'a person' and 'a person.' Lucas did not give me a chance to explain that Alex is a peaceful person who treats me with dignity and respect, who looks out for me, who has a genuine interest in my needs. With Alex, I feel young, alive, and vibrant. I feel whole and energetic. Conversely, when I am with Lucas, I feel empty, wasted, and lifeless.

A Butterfly

Lucas renewed his visa at the border and left me at Alex's place. Then I was able to focus on my typing and Alex:

3/2/12 – Alex went to town early this morning to bring back one of those 5-gallon bottles of drinking water from the border. On the bus! When he returned, he teased me, with a twinkle in his eye, "I saw a lot of pretty women out there. I am glad I do not need to look anymore!"

I objected, "No, you must look at them! I am a butterfly, remember?" With a confident smile and a twinkle in my own eye, I continued, "I'm a shining blue one!"

My Mountain

3/10/12 – It feels wonderful to be back on the mountain and able to enjoy the solitude, silence, and natural splendor of this place. I am 'home'.

Males Again

3/12/12 – Had my first good night's rest in a long time last night. Carlos seemed very happy to see me this morning. I excitedly showed him the book manuscript that I had typed and printed at Alex's. It's finally starting to look like a book. I am not sure he understood the significance of what I was showing him, but I tried to tell him that it's the story of my struggle with depression and how the Eternal God we both love and serve has blessed me with new hope.

Horror of horrors, Lucas came up the mountain to my private little retreat today, totally uninvited. He knows I want to be alone up here. Maybe I am making a big deal out of nothing, but I feel completely vulnerable now that he knows he can come up any time he feels like it. Grrrrr. I thought that living here on this mountain I could feel safe from unwanted visitors. I feel like my 'space' has been invaded and could be again at any time. When will I be strong enough to tell him not to come up here?

Solitude

3/16/12, 2 a.m. – Eternal God, I am so happy to be alone with You again. Sometimes I feel like I am an oddball for needing space and time alone. People look at me as if I am crazy and tell me I will get over it, but is it any different from Moses being in the wilderness for 40 years or Your Son being alone with You for 40 days? I yearn for You, thirst for You, long to be one with You. Your approval is everything to me. Knowing that You love me is essential. Speak to my heart, beloved Yahweh, and let me comfort Yours.

8:30 p.m. – Thinking about Alex and his sensitive soul. I do not want him to become another statistic in my list of failed relationships.

3/17/12, 4:30 a.m. – I miss Alex, my prayer partner. We did not have long morning and evening worships, but they were definitely part of our time together. He is the first man I know who has an active devotional life, a habit of spending time with God. He does not just wish he had a relationship with God; he has one. And he comes forth from his room radiant and at peace. I want what he has – that connection with the Divine One, that holy experience.

Gathering Momentum

By this time, my butterfly wings were fully dry and fully functioning. Writing the book manuscript had been therapeutic for my wounded soul, and I was preparing for take-off. I was ready to tackle Lucas:

3/25/12 – I had yet another altercation with Lucas down at Tim's place this morning. He insisted that I should bring his cell phone up to my mountain retreat "for emergencies".

After his speech, I screamed to myself, "Just get out of my life, Lucas! I don't want your cell phone. Sure, it could save my life, but I want nothing else from you! Your gifts always have strings attached. I deserve better. I don't want to give myself away for free anymore. I want to spend the time the Eternal has given me with people who enrich my life. Thanks, but no thanks!"

Something Has Changed

By this point, I was reluctantly realizing that something was different about Alex than early on. He often seemed withdrawn, and from what he said, this was true of him whether or not I was around. I recognized this symptom of depression (and there were others) and felt increasing tension in our relationship:

3/26/12 – I am on the bus returning from the border yet again. It always feels good to accomplish something while I am there. After all, that is why I take these excursions to Alex's house – so I can type in peace and quiet and comfort (and, of course, see Alex).

Alex was in 'shut down mode' again for the past several days. More and more, he reminds me of one of my other men as far as his introversion goes. I feel that I overstayed my welcome again. It seems that he retreats into his shell when my presence is overwhelming for him. Even though it seems that he is far away sometimes, I am still grateful for his friendship. The only time we connected the entire week was during our shared meditation, which is always a beautiful experience.

Lightning-quick Decisions

The day after my arrival back at the hut on the mountain, my cozy little world was turned upside down once again. I wrote about it a week later:

4/4/12 – The day after I arrived back from my most recent trek to the border, I received some not-so-pleasant information. Tim raised the subject of the family's intentions for the rancho where I am currently staying, my healing sanctuary. Basically, it sounded like if I were not able or willing to become part of a team who would go up to the house only on a 'rotating schedule,' responsible for collecting admission to the waterfall, etc. – I would need to leave.

I thought about this for a few moments and then informed Tim sorrowfully, "Thanks, but I'd rather not be a part of a team at this point. I am still working on my book full time, so transitioning between the rancho and my tent down here would not work. I need a regular place to hang my hat right now. Thanks for your kindness, but I will look for another place to stay."

So here I am, homeless once more. Maybe I can find a cheap place to rent in another country in Central America that has a lower cost of living? I could probably find a part-time job teaching English as a second language to pay rent and buy bananas. When I told Lucas about Tim's conversation, he showed no surprise and bluntly stated, "It doesn't matter whether or not you move to a different country. You're dead to me now anyway."

Later – When I hiked up the mountain for the last time today, I shed a few tears. The tears were not because I will miss my private sanctuary, although I know I will, having become very attached to the beauty, tranquility, and solitude of the place. No, it's the stress of trying to find a new place to stay.

Evening – I am feeling better, although I am still discouraged about looking for another place to stay while I finish my book. I put my evening candle beside the SHINE sign on the shelf tonight and walked around the deck singing "Shine, Jesus, Shine."

Eternal God, You have promised that You are with me and I have nothing to fear. Be with me so I will not be afraid. Strengthen my little faith.

Adios

4/6/12 – I have already started packing my stuff for my trip across the border so I can vacate this house on Sunday. Thankfully, I do not have much up here so it's quite simple.

Things were moving quickly now, so quickly that I did not even have time to journal my bittersweet thoughts about leaving my mountain sanctuary, anxiety about what the future might hold, and sketchy plans to stay in Central America and try to make it on my own. On the other hand, as a butterfly with newly tested wings, I was eager to strike out on my own, with my hand placed firmly in the Master's:

4/9/12 – On the bus again, heading back to the border, probably for the last time. Although in one sense it feels good to be leaving the place where I keep bumping into Lucas and stressing myself out, it's bittersweet to say farewell to the other friends I have made in this country.

The past 24 hours have been upsetting for me emotionally – I am exhausted. It's the third morning in a row that I have been up at 3 a.m., but finally, I am in a healthy place, at least mentally.

When I called Alex to let him know I will be passing through his town on my way to a neighboring country, I asked if I could take a little detour to his house.

He said in his usual, peaceable way, "You can stay with me until you decide what you're doing next. One day at a time, Brenna. Hang in there – it will be over soon."

Now that is support! Alex knows I am a butterfly, and he knows I have nothing, yet he still said he would be happy to see me when I get down to the border. And the message on my heart for Lucas: "The Almighty is our Witness and our Judge."

Is this chapter of my life over yet? Not yet, but it will be soon. I am going to stop writing now, breathe deeply, and enjoy the scenery from the bus windows.

Airport Update

Ten days after I left my Eden, the burden to complete my book manuscript and get it into the hands of hurting women caused me to reverse my decision to stay in Central America as explained further below:

4/19/12 – I am not sure what I am doing at the airport, but here I sit waiting for my flight back to the U.S.

After a one-day vow of silence and several days of fasting and prayer at Alex's house, it has become clear to me that the best thing I can do for myself, and my healing is to accept my sister's invitation to stay with her short term. At least I will have a roof over my head and food to eat. And perhaps most importantly, I will be in a position to finally finish this book manuscript.

The burden of my heart is to provide a voice for frustrated victims of PMDD like me, to bring hope to those suffering from the symptoms of this disorder, as well as for their loved ones. I am following my heart, my own voice for a change, which I believe is the Father's will for me. It's delightful!

Alex and I spent some bittersweet days together, getting further acquainted yet fully aware that I would be leaving Central America. He lives in the 'now' so enjoyed my company regardless. I am so thankful to know him. Now it's onward and upward for me, starting all over once again.

Eternal God, grant me wisdom to know how to help other women with this book and receive healing for my own heart as I reflect on Your many blessings. I know the exciting journey with You will continue if I remain obedient and faithful. I love you, Yahweh!

Chapter 11 – What is PMDD?

PMDD (Premenstrual Dysphoric Disorder) is a relatively rare psychiatric disorder affecting approximately 3-8% of menstruating women. Because it is a major mood disturbance, a recognized mental disorder on the American Psychiatric Association's list, including it on this list further alienates and stigmatizes those who suffer from it. However, recognizing PMDD as a distinct diagnostic entity may benefit the relatively small number of women who suffer from it by providing them with validation that it is not 'all in their heads.'

Women with PMDD experience severe and debilitating symptoms which are predominantly psychological in nature such as irritability, depression, weepiness, mood swings, insomnia, fatigue, and social withdrawal. These women suffer so severely that work productivity, social activities, and family and personal relationships are seriously affected.

The disabling symptoms of PMDD predictably return monthly. They are present during the 14 days from ovulation until the first day of menstruation (luteal phase). Then there is a symptom-free time during the week of menses plus the following week (follicular phase).

The Difference between PMS and PMDD

PMDD exhibits many of the same symptoms as PMS but in much more severe, disabling forms, especially episodes of significant depression. Simply put, comparing PMS and PMDD is similar to comparing a mild headache with a full-blown migraine.

Possible Causes

As with PMS, the exact cause for PMDD is largely unknown or at least poorly understood. Some studies show a likely correlation between PMDD and stress, resulting in a blunted sympathetic nervous system response which includes low levels of serotonin, a brain chemical that helps transmit nerve signals. This abnormal central nervous system function is likely caused by genetic factors. Simply put, there is a strong genetic connection in PMDD, a high genetic vulnerability which can contribute to susceptibility to PMDD. Complex psychological, biological, environmental, and social factors play a role as well.

PMDD Awareness

I read once that something like 8 out of 10 women do not know that severe premenstrual problems have been officially classified as PMDD, nor do they know that such problems can be diagnosed and treated. (I used to be one of those women.) To make matters worse, lack of awareness is closely followed by skepticism regarding the very existence of this disorder. And if a woman's medical practitioner does not believe it exists, where can she turn for support and possible medical intervention?

Diagnosis and Treatment

Diagnosing and treating PMS and PMDD is complex, as many women who have premenstrual complaints also have preexisting conditions which get worse during those two weeks prior to menstruation. In addition, currently there is no noninvasive biomarker test to evaluate menstrual cycle fluctuations. In other words, other than conservative treatment options such as stress management and cognitive behavioral therapy, and extreme options such as a hysterectomy, the selective serotonin reuptake inhibitors (SSRI'S) appear to be the best treatment option in severe cases, and even these medications are often ineffective.

Knowledge is Powerful

To 'know the foe' is to give yourself a precious gift: confidence to deal with 'it' (in this case, PMDD) instead of allowing 'it' to control you. Awareness of the possible causes of PMDD, its symptoms, its triggers in her situation, etc., provides a woman with a powerful and critical choice. By knowing what she is up against, she can choose to fight or to acquiesce, to battle the foe or to just ride the waves as best she can. 'Riding the waves' simply means surrounding herself with a safe environment and safe people and waiting out the storm. Sometimes that environment may be her own private dungeon where it's cold and dark and lonely, but it's safe there. After all, even if a woman chooses to accept the darkness in the dungeon for a little while, she is still choosing to fight. She is fighting by *not* fighting, so she is still in the battle.

Symptoms of PMDD

PMDD symptoms are like those of PMS but are *much more severe and persistent*. These may include:

- markedly depressed mood
- overwhelming hopelessness
- suicide ideation
- increased interpersonal conflicts
- increased need for emotional closeness

- clumsiness
- prolonged periods of weepiness
- decreased productivity at work or school
- avoidance of social activities
- marked affective lability (mood swings)
- persistent and marked anger, rage, or irritability
- debilitating fatigue

Friends and Family

Do your best to show your loved one that you support her by being sensitive to her moods and needs to whatever degree you can. Keep in mind that PMDD is *her* problem, not yours, although you will definitely share the effects of some of the symptoms.

As one author points out, "You have to allow other people their pain. If you do not, you risk losing everything for nothing, because anything you can do from outside will never work. You could end up throwing your own life away; and your relative or partner, at the end of it, will still be ill: a double defeat."[4]

Remember to take care of yourself. As the caregiver, it's vital that you get out and talk to people who are well, if only to remind yourself what it's like to have relationships with living people. Your partner with PMDD may mutate into a corpse every month, but you can maintain balance in your own life by taking care of your own needs. It requires a lot of energy to be cheerful around ill people.

---

[4] Lewis, 124-125.

Chapter 12 – What is H.O.P.E.?

While I was living in my jungle haven, I discovered an acronym that helped me remember some of the keys to keeping my head above water during my cyclical depression:

Hold God's Hand, He is Holding Yours
Open the Door to New Possibilities
Practice the Laws of Health
Establish a Healing Environment

Perhaps they will serve as timely reminders for you as well, so now we will look at each one of them more closely:

Hold God's Hand, He is Holding Yours:
A Place of Power

Is there anything as delightful as walking with a toddler who looks up at you and trustingly puts his hand in yours? An innocent gesture such as this will warm any heart. Is it any wonder, then, that the One who created us takes great pleasure in walking with His children? Because He made you and knows you, you can be confident that it's safe to reach up and take His strong hand in your own.

Therefore, you begin your healing by recognizing the importance of being connected with the Eternal God, depending on a heavenly force that is far beyond human.

Even more importantly, rest assured that when you cannot hold His hand, He is always holding yours. When the floor drops out and the wild winds blow, He is with you.

Open the Door to New Possibilities:
A Place of Purpose

Having a purpose in life is vital for anyone living with depression. I believe the Eternal One has called every person on this planet to a special purpose – a function, a duty, a distinct role chosen for each one of us to fulfill based on our special skills, abilities, and passions – and it's up to each of us to discover and fulfill that purpose.

Tim and Diana provided that opportunity to me when they offered to let me stay in their healing garden sanctuary. Accepting that offer gave me the opportunity to escape a stressful situation and live in my 'peaceful place' for a little while. For the first time in years, I saw glimmers of hope for changes in my living situation and solutions to my seemingly perpetual quandaries. Like a hungry child grabbing a warm oatmeal cookie, I seized the opportunity. Then I flew!

Practice the Laws of Health:
A Place of Proper Habits

The laws of health cover everything from diet and exercise to sleep hygiene and the proper use of water. Do not take these natural laws for granted.

For example, in my situation in Central America, I had access to a cold shower with water piped down from a mountain stream. I usually jumped under the icy flow of water after a long hike to make it more bearable as my body was already overheated by that time. Sometimes I went for a nippy dip in the crystal-clear waterfall pools. Both activities stimulated my skin and organs. These natural forms of hydrotherapy undoubtedly aided in my recovery.

Of course, hydrotherapy is not for everyone, but it has numerous health benefits.

Establish a Healing Environment:
A Place of Peace

The word *healing* means *to restore to health or wholeness* – whole in mind, body, and spirit. To deliberately create a peaceful place for ourselves where healing can take place requires some thought about what type of environment is best for us, remembering to consider sounds, aromas, and touch sensations that will nourish our soul.

Something that has been enormously helpful to me in recent years is a *coping kit*, a *beauty box* of sorts, a container of gadgets and gizmos and lists of activities to do when I am at the end of my rope. Some are for general dark days; others are for when I am literally at the end of my rope such as a suicide hotline number (taped to the top of the lid so it's easy to find). The items you choose to keep in your coping kit are going to be different from anyone else's. Keep them practical and keep them personal.

Chapter 13 – Living with H.O.P.E.

Healed for a Purpose

I still find it incredible that those dark days have not reappeared for several months. To most people, that may not seem like a great length of time, but for a person suffering from cyclical depression and the other symptoms of PMDD, it is more than a lifetime of joy!

Since escaping that dark dungeon, I have been able to:

- make plans ahead of time without fear of fatigue or weepiness
- take care of my needs without needing to ask for assistance
- walk for an hour or more without fear of running out of steam

I am no longer afraid that the unexplained fury of Irritable Iris or Raging Rhonda will attack me unawares or that I will proverbially 'remove someone's head' if I get angry. By the grace of God, any anger I now experience is explainable and controllable.

It's exciting to be able to look forward now. Even though I may not have the financial resources I need to achieve some of my goals, at least I can visualize them. My experience with PMDD and its accompanying symptoms serves to remind me that a woman can lose her health, husband, friends, family, income, home, life goals, and dreams and still rebound to live a rewarding and meaningful life. I thank the Eternal for mercy and resilience.

Recently, a doctor friend of mine stated that the longer we live, the more we experience of God's goodness. A lightbulb went on in my mind as I carried that thought forward: therefore, I will taste more of God's goodness if I live a long life. I am hungry for His goodness, and this is perfect motivation to stay alive!

Finally – Hope!

There are thousands of women silently suffering in the dungeon of depression, whether from PMDD or some other cause. Maybe you are one of them. Perhaps you're searching for light but do not know where to turn. My life has been restored to me; I was healed for a purpose. It is only by the grace of God that I am alive today. With eternal gratitude to the Eternal God, I have shared my story of hope in this book.

"He alone is my rock, my salvation, and my fortress" (Psalm *62:2a*).

Epilogue

Sometimes I feel disappointed that I have not found a solution for the symptoms of PMDD. I'd love to be able to say that I have. However, I have found something infinitely greater than a life without depression or moodiness or tearful weeks or persistent irritability or any of the other symptoms I suffer – I have found *Someone*. I have learned that Yahweh, the Eternal God, was holding onto me through all those years of pain when I had no hope. I am learning to thrive when there is water and sunlight, and to close my petals and rest when the environment is not conducive to life; to take butterfly-flights when there is wind to carry me, and to flutter and 'free-fall' when there is less than a breeze. Ah, the marvelous mercy of Yahweh!

Where are They Now?

Tim and Diana, who blessed me with the opportunity to escape to the secluded mountain paradise, complete with organic garden, waterfall, hiking trails, and gardener, continue to share their sanctuary in Central America with those in need of spiritual, physical, and mental healing.

Lucas recently returned from Central America and is busier than a one-eyed cat watching two mouse holes. He is a jungle monkey, and I predict that he'll return to the tropics next winter.

Alex and I correspond frequently. He continues to spend the better part of his days outdoors caring for the hundreds of varieties of fruit trees, flowers, and exotic foliage that he planted on his property.

www.ingramcontent.com/pod-product-compliance
Lightning Source LLC
Chambersburg PA
CBHW070835160726
48004CB00001B/394